RAISED BED GARDENING FOR BEGINNERS

HOW TO BUILD AND GROW VEGETABLES IN YOUR OWN RAISED BED GARDEN

SUSAN WRIGHT

PUBLISHING FORTE

INTRODUCTION

Raised bed gardening is a fun alternative to traditional gardening that offers a number of benefits. If you look closely, you might notice raised bed gardens creeping into or taking over people's gardens recently. Gardening is, in general, a pleasurable and productive activity. Growing your own food has its own set of advantages and might help you avoid boredom.

To begin, raised bed gardening is concerned with raised gardens. A raised garden is a garden that is planted inside a frame and ranges in height from a few inches to a few feet. Stone, wood, or whatever else you wish to use might be used to make these frames. This may appear strange at first, but it has its benefits.

The first is that it is easier to work on for seniors and other persons who have bad backs. There would be no need to stoop over because the garden will be as high as you want it. This type of gardening is suitable for persons who use wheelchairs or have limited mobility, not to mention that the quality of the plants and foods produced by these garden kinds is far superior.

The soil in a raised garden is not as compacted as ground soil because it should not be on the bottom, and no one steps on it. This is another benefit of raised bed gardening over traditional gardening. When soil isn't compacted, plant roots can stretch out more easily, allowing the plant to grow and survive at a greater level than it could on the ground. As a result, raised bed gardens may outperform traditional gardens in this regard.

It's not a competition or anything, but it may be crucial for those of us who develop our own cuisine. In these kinds of gardens, you can build anything you want; it doesn't have to be flowers. Fruits, vegetables, and just about anything else that grows in-ground soil will thrive in a raised garden. It's easy to see how this could be a fun task to have around the house or a way to teach your kids about gardening.

Another thing to keep in mind is that raised gardening cannot be done outside. You can have a garden indoors as long as you have sufficient sunlight and access to water. This isn't a new concept; many of us now have indoor gardens. This may make it easier to manage, especially if you don't need to leave the house or if it's raining outdoors.

Raised bed gardening is a fun alternative to traditional gardening. Raised bed gardens are simpler to maintain and are ideal for persons in poor health or older. They also create wonderful one-of-a-kind items and conversation starters. You can grow your fruits and veggies inside your home, just like any other garden, but I wouldn't recommend growing maize on a waist-high counter. It could get a little crowded unless you have a really high ceiling.

Raised beds are becoming increasingly popular among gardeners of all skill levels. You may learn how easy and convenient it is to cultivate with a gorgeous planter bed whether you are an expert, a beginner, a senior citizen, or even a child.

You accomplish various things when you increase the bed of your planting surface. Lifting an elderly citizen's planting surface can mean the difference between them continuing to enjoy their lifetime hobby of flower or vegetable gardening. This is also useful for relieving back and neck tension, which can become excruciating in certain elderly people. You can make the garden more comfortable for you by lifting the planter to eye level and arm's length. Lifting the bed provides a regulated and easy-to-maintain space for children and even novice gardeners. You have a smaller space that requires less weeding and trimming rather than a large space that can easily become out of control. Raised bed gardening is quite practical, according to expert gardeners. When you lift an area to expand its depth, you create an environment where the earth remains loose and deep rather than compressed. Plants thrive in this type of habitat because they may sink their roots deep into the soil. In addition, many planting beds are composed of recycled materials and insect-resistant timber components. This makes organic gardening a viable option for you at home, regardless of your skill level.

Raised garden beds provide benefits such as less weeding, improved soil conditions, and fewer backaches. Learn how to produce flowers and food in your backyard or on your deck with attractive garden beds that are raised for easier maintenance and greater growth.

1
WHAT IS RAISED BED GARDENING?

Raised bed gardening is a simple technique that can improve the health and productivity of your garden. Raised beds have better soil structure and drainage, allowing the soil to warm up earlier in the season, and giving you a head start on spring.

RAISED BED gardens are an ideal way to grow vegetables and small fruit. They are elevated a few inches or more above the soil level and just wide enough to reach across by hand. Plants can be grouped in a bed with permanent walkways on either side. The soil does not get compacted since the soil in which plants are grown never walked on.

IF YOU ENJOY EATING FRESH, organic vegetables but dislike the prospect of weeding or running up a large water bill with a standard row garden, square foot gardening is for you. A four-foot raised garden bed with four side panels, and no bottom is used for square foot planting. To lay the foundation, you'll need to lay down a weed barrier. Then you fill the bed with a special soil mix that includes three equal parts vermiculite (to keep moisture in the soil), peat moss (to keep the soil light and loose for drainage), and compost (for nutrients). All of these can be found at your local nursery or garden center. If you're in a hurry to get started on your raised bed garden, just buy commercial compost for the time being. However, starting your organic compost for later would be well worth your time. It's a terrific method to save money on commercial fertilizer while also utilizing the nutrients in your kitchen, vegetable leftovers, and grass clippings.

An enclosed compost tumbler is the most convenient way to make compost. Then you won't have to deal with an open compost heap's ugly mess, stench, or insects. Look for a composter with a large, removable top for easy access and a crank that is simple to turn. Because it takes a few months for organic scraps to decompose into a rich fertilizer for your plants, you'll want to begin your homemade compost going as soon as possible.

Now, because you've got your own soil mix contained within the walls of this raised bed, you'll gain instant and noticeable benefits that you wouldn't get from traditional row planting. This garden bed's dirt will never be walked or kneeled on; thus, it will never become compacted. This has a number of benefits for you. To begin with, no rototilling will be required next season, and there will be less watering. Because of the loose soil, proper water drainage and moisture retention will be possible. Another benefit of keeping your plants in a 4-ft square bed is that you can simply access any part of your garden from the side of the bed without having to enter the garden. Isn't that a more practical method to plan a garden layout?

PLANT SPACING in square foot gardening is done on a grid, with a different type of plant in each square foot. It's a good idea to mark out this grid with twine before planting to guarantee correct plant spacing. The number of plants you insert in each square is determined by the plant's mature size. Because tomato plants are prolific vine plants, only one tomato plant per square foot is recommended. However, each square can hold up to four strawberry plants. Squash and cucumbers, for example, need to be grown vertically on a very solid frame since their runners take up so much area. You'll need an extra-deep bed with at least 12 inches of soil for deep-rooted plants like potatoes or carrots.

YOU CAN MAKE your own raised garden bed or purchase a ready-made kit. Commercial raised bed kits are convenient because the panels are pre-measured, and all of the essential hardware is included.

PLASTIC-PANELED RAISED garden bed kits have some advantages over wooden garden beds. They aren't prone to warping, decay, or attracting insects. Plastic boards are convenient because they are lightweight and smooth, and there are no splinters to worry about. In less than an hour, you can create a plastic raised garden bed with interlocking panels. Some of them come with an "early start" clear vinyl container, which is particularly useful in places with a short growing season. These raised garden kits include beds that can be used individually or double-stacked to make extra-deep beds. The interlocking construction also allows you to dismantle and transfer the bed if necessary swiftly.

How to Get Started

The majority of individuals who have gardens in their backyards take their good soil for granted. Sure, they may need to add some fertilizer to help their flowers or veggies grow more quickly, but for the most part, everything is running well.

RAISED BED GARDENING IS, fortunately, a simple and inexpensive way to get started. The first step is to mark out the area of your yard where you want to plant your plants. Before you do this, think about what you want to grow (and how much) so you can figure out how much space you'll need as well as the overall size and shape of the space. Also, now is the time to consider how much sunlight your chosen plants will require to thrive and make sure you arrange the beds in an appropriate location.

AFTER YOU'VE DECIDED on your preliminary designs, you'll need to decide on the type of raised bed gardening containers you want to utilize. There are numerous solutions available, all of which perform admirably, so the final decision is mostly a matter of personal preference. If you only want to do the bare minimum, throw up some decent dirt directly on top of your existing soil. Many people prefer this technique since it only takes around six inches of new soil (or less) to flourish most flowers or veggies.

OTHERS LIKE to cultivate on a raised bed that is little more than a plain wooden box. They just tie a few wood planks in the ground around the soil mounds they intend to use as a garden. For something a little more elaborate, you can purchase various stones or bricks to surround your garden and give it a more exquisite look. These items are available at your local plant nursery or home improvement retailer, and they are well worth the extra expense and work.

THAT'S all there is to it when it comes to preparing your yard for raised bed gardening. Once the actual beds are in place, you can simply plant as you would if you were planting straight into the ground. Watering, weeding, and other routine upkeep are all quite similar, so you won't have to worry about learning new skills or anything.

The Benefits of Raised Bed Gardening

Vegetables planted in a raised bed tend to grow larger, healthier and have a stronger flavor. Why not give a raised bed vegetable garden a try this growing season if you haven't already?

MOUNDED RAISED vegetable gardens to allow you to concentrate soil amendments, water levels, and fertilizer into a smaller space. Dirt mounds that have been divided into rows. The mounds should be at least 12 inches tall, but they may need to be taller to allow adequate root growth depending on the plants being cultivated.

SOIL AMENDMENT

The soil on one's property is frequently unsuitable for growing healthy plants. As a result, many people will opt to build a raised garden. This permits the individual to alter the soil by tilling in organic matter such as compost or other organic matter.

Rich, well-draining soil is required for the growth of vegetables. There will be times when the present ground in the raised garden will need to be dug out and totally rebuilt. If the present soil is classified as "clay," for example, all of it must be removed and replaced with well-draining soil. Soil can be purchased from companies that specialize in landscaping supplies.

Watering a Vegetable Garden in a Raised Bed

- *Downspouts System*

Watering a raised bed vegetable garden can be done in a variety of ways. Take advantage of one home's downspout system by directing rainfall flow into the vegetable garden and allowing it to soak in and around the bed. This is an environmentally friendly way to water the raised bed vegetable garden.

- *Water Hoses System*

If a raised garden is developed in a location where using one's home downspout is not practical, a water hose can achieve a similar function. If this becomes the preferred approach, make careful to keep the water flow under control. Allowing the water to progressively fill the base of your raised bed vegetable garden before turning it off is preferable to flooding the bed. The soil at the bed's base should never be "washed away" by water. If there isn't enough rain, this method is a wonderful backup plan for the downspout system.

. . .

BOTH OF THE ways mentioned will maintain the plant roots above the water level. This provides an atmosphere in which the plants benefit from deep watering, allowing them to reach for the water at the base. In the long term, this strategy produces a very healthy plant.

- *Sprinklers System*

WATERING A RAISED bed garden with a sprinkler system is also a good idea. Depending on your budget, there are various variants and styles of sprinkler systems to accomplish a healthy growing raised vegetable garden efficiently. The most expensive option is to have a sprinkler system professionally installed and set on a timer. However, a decent quality portable sprinkler that attaches to the end of a water hose and produces amazing results may be purchased for under $20. However, make sure to water the raised bed garden on a regular and timely basis.

Fertilizing a Vegetable Garden in a Raised Bed

Fertilizer is a natural or manufactured material that is put to or distributed on the soil to help it stimulate plant development. Fertilizing a raised bed vegetable garden is essential for generating beautiful and nutritious produce. The sort of fertilizer required is determined by the veggies that are grown. If you're new to vegetable gardening or aren't sure which fertilizer is ideal for your plants, please seek advice from a professional or someone who is familiar with growing veggies.

2
RAISED BED GARDEN IDEAS

For areas with difficult-to-work soil and inadequate drainage, a raised bed garden is the ideal option. There are several raised bed gardening ideas to choose from. To make your garden unique and stand out from the crowd, use your creativity.

Raised gardens are available in a variety of forms, sizes, and quantities. You have the option of having a single huge garden or two or three smaller gardens. Smaller gardens appear to be easier to maintain.

Try shapes other than the standard rectangular one to add style to your outdoor space. Hexagons may bring a lot of interest to a space while yet being simple to layout and design.

There are a variety of materials to choose from. Walking around your local garden shops and home improvement stores might provide you with raised bed gardening ideas. Choose something that will go well with your house and the landscaping around it.

Wood is a popular material for raised bed gardeners. It is widely available and simple to use. Railroad ties have a rustic look, whereas planed timber has a more polished appearance.

Although pressure-treated timber lasts longer than untreated wood, it is not the safest option for growing vegetables in the garden. Non-treated timbers like redwood and cedar last longer than treated woods, so they'd be a better choice for growing food close by.

Many different sorts of raised bed gardening ideas may be created using stone. It also lasts considerably longer than any other type of wood and is readily available. Depending on the style you want to create, you can use it with or without mortar.

Concrete in ornamental shapes may be found at garden stores at a reasonable price. This can be done with or without the use of mortar. If you enjoy the notion of repurposing materials, you may create a distinctive look by stacking shattered concrete pieces.

Brick is a great material to use when building a raised bed garden. It gives the entire space a very formal and polished appearance.

. . .

THE ONLY DISADVANTAGE is the amount of time and effort necessary to install it. A mortar is required. It would be beneficial to have it installed by a professional.

ANOTHER FACTOR TO consider when it comes to raised bed gardening ideas is the sort of plants to use. If the only aim is to be ornamental, rich green foliage, blooming plants and shrubs may be used. Choose plants that thrive in your area. Consider if the garden is in full sun, partial shade, or a combination of both.

IN RAISED BEDS, vegetables are a popular plant to cultivate. They truly benefit from high-quality soil and great drainage. The majority of veggies are suitable for this sort of garden. When choosing which kinds to plant, keep your available space in mind.

Raised Bed Garden Soil

There's a lot of discussion over what kind of soil is ideal for a raised garden bed. Organic gardeners improve the soil; they already have to create their own soil. When clay and compost are combined, the resulting soil can be the greatest you've ever had.

CLAY SOIL MAY PROVIDE numerous benefits to an organic garden that no other soil can, and when combined with compost, the results can be priceless, ranging from plant-feeding to novel insect control strategies. When clay is added to plants or soil in an organic garden, it may give a variety of benefits.

. . .

MANY ESSENTIAL ELEMENTS and metals necessary for plant growth, such as iron, calcium, potassium, and trace quantities of other organic compounds, are found in clay soil and are not found in many other soil types. When added to the composting process, clay can improve the potency of the compost.

BECAUSE THE CLAY particles are negatively charged, they may attract and hold onto positively charged substances like ammonium, calcium, magnesium, potassium, and other trace elements or absorb them. Because of its capacity to absorb these important plant nutrients, clay soil is relatively productive.

IN A CLAY SOIL MANAGEMENT STRATEGY, compost is essential. Compost is highly resistant to further breakdown due to its humified form, low concentration of oxidizable carbon, and accessible nitrogen. It is not for nutrient value that compost is added to any soil. It's for improving the physical characteristics of soil over time by boosting organic carbon, and humic matter stabilized organic matter content.

COMPOST PROVIDES nutritious food for earthworms and other helpful bacteria. These organisms and microbes indicate that compost is a regenerative living substance that contributes to a healthy soil ecosystem. They are required to naturally work the soil by digesting organic matter and releasing nutrients as they pass through it. Composted soil helps to reduce disease and pest issues that may otherwise take over your garden.

. . .

THE PH of the soil improves when it is modified with compost. Nutrients are accessible to most vegetable garden plants when the pH is between 5.5 and 7.5. When combined with soil, completed compost generally has a pH of 6.0 - 8.0, with 7.0 being neutral, allowing it to retain the pH at ideal levels for nutrient availability.

CLAY SOIL and compost will work together to give many benefits that no other soil combination can. Compost binds to clay particles, creating bigger particles with more air space between them when applied as a soil amendment with clay. Surface water drainage and air penetration are improved as a result of the wider gaps.

Raised Bed Garden Soil Preparation

Layering based on soil type:
Different soil types necessitate different forms of layering. Sandy soils will require a mix with half the amount of sand and twice the amount of peat. Sandy soils become more drought-resistant and may retain moisture better when this top layer is applied. A layer of one part peat, four parts sand, and two parts loam are required for clayey soil because it aids root development and provides for improved drainage.

INGREDIENTS MUST BE WELL blended before being uniformly applied to the soil. After that, use the back of a rake or a stiff broom to stir the mixture into the surface. The grass will not be covered until this method is followed.

. . .

You should not rush the application since patience is required to prepare the soil for a raised bed garden. The soil in the garden might get compacted with larger particles at times. In this situation, an even or thin coating of sand must be uniformly placed across the layer.

Layering yearly:

Aerate the soil before adding the top layer of sand. This is primarily done to ensure that air can easily circulate around the roots of the grass. Air may readily travel around the roots when air channels are created in the soil, which can be done by removing the cores.

Taking out the cores is similar to installing spikes or coring an apple. Raising your garden bed is important since it keeps your grass healthy all year round. The process may not take much of your time, and if you need to hire a gardener, it will be well worth your time. After all, the garden must look healthy because it is part of your home environment.

Raised Bed Soil Mix Recipe

Now it's time to get down to business with your basic starting recipe. Fill in the blanks with the goods listed below in the anticipated quantities. This is only a base mixture. Depending on your local environment and what you want to produce, feel free to add or remove extra modifications.

Various plants may require different pH values in the soil. As a result, constantly test your final soil and modify it to match the environment of what you're growing. But, for the most part, this blend should set you off to a fantastic start for many seasons to come.

50% of Compost

Good-quality organic compost should make up 50% of your raised bed. Compost sellers who can't tell you what their compost is made of should be avoided.

IF THEY INCLUDE grass in their mix, double-check that any grass clippings added to the compost haven't been treated with fertilizers or pesticides that might harm your plants. You should aim for a 4:1 ratio of browns (carbon) to greens in your compost (nitrogen).

GREENS INCLUDE GRASS CLIPPINGS, manure, and food scraps, while browns include well-rotted leaves and weed-free straw. You may produce your own or buy some from a garden shop or a local provider. Compost not only adds a ton of nutrients to your soil, but it also gives it structure, helping it to hold moisture better while still allowing for appropriate drainage and providing the ideal habitat for garden aids like earthworms to thrive.

40% of Good Topsoil

Good-quality topsoil should make up another 40% of your soil mix. Squeeze a handful of dirt into your fist to test it. When you open your palm, the dirt should stick together, but it should also quickly fall apart when you touch it.

. . .

If the soil isn't holding together, there's probably too much sand in it. It may cause drainage difficulties if it does not break apart readily. If you have adequate native soil on your site, you may save money by incorporating it into the bottom section of the bed with your compost.

If you have naturally heavy clay soil, make careful to mix it in well to avoid a poorly draining layer at the bottom.

5% of Coconut Coir

Coconut coir doesn't offer much nutrition to the soil, but it does function as a sustainable soil aerator, holding both air and water in the soil at the same time. These characteristics can help to break up hard or compacted soil while also improving the structure of your raised bed and its capacity to retain water.

This is especially useful in dry areas where there are frequent droughts or water restrictions.

5% of Nutritional Soil Bomb Mixture

The last 5% should consist of a mix of things that will assist rocket your seeds or seedlings to the finish line while preserving a strong root system and a variety of nutrients. Keep in mind that plants get a lot of their nourishment from the earth.

The better your soil, the better your fruits and veggies will taste and maybe have more nutritional content.

. . .

Castings of Worms

Worms will hopefully make your garden bed their home over time, especially because you've created the ideal climate for them. Worms consume organic debris in your raised bed and excrete nutrient-dense castings. Most garden centers sell these castings in sacks, or you may get them online.

With worm castings, a little goes a long way. You may also use worm castings at the bottom of your planting holes to direct nutrients to your growing area and save money.

Compost Mushrooms

Compost created from mushrooms is not the same as mushroom compost. It is a byproduct of mushroom cultivation and is composed of the mushrooms' materials, such as corncobs or hay. Mushroom compost adds potassium, nitrogen, and a trace of phosphorus to your soil mixture.

Rock Dust (Azomite)

Rock dust enriches your raised bed soil with critical minerals and trace elements that are often lacking in today's soil mixes. Azomite users also claim better-tasting fruits and greater harvests in terms of both number and size.

Mycorrhizae

Your compost or topsoil mix may already include mycorrhizae. If not, these beneficial fungi can be added to your soil mix. In return for extracting carbon from the plant, these fungi colonize the roots of your plants and help them better absorb nutrients from the soil.

NITROGEN, phosphorus, and other critical micronutrients are more readily available as a result.

Which Materials are Safe for Containing your Beds?

The size and shape of your project will most likely be determined by the materials you use. More significantly, several of you voiced worries and inquired about the safety of certain materials. This is where everything may go awry. There is a lot of contradicting information out there, and there is surprisingly little research on the different materials that may be used.

WHAT IS the significance of materials? To begin with, the resources you employ will be very near to your food crop. Roots and vegetation will very certainly come into touch with your material surface on a frequent basis.

SECOND, the soil you use in your bed will need to be wet, and the outside surfaces of your bed will be exposed to the sun for long periods of time. When exposed to continuous dampness and sunshine, most materials deteriorate.

REGARDLESS, **here are some advantages and disadvantages of the materials you could be considering:**

- *Raw Wood*

BLACK WALNUT, cypress, cedar, redwood, oak, black locust, or osage orange are the greatest sorts of untreated wood. These are noted for their rot resistance and may endure for years, especially in damp environments.

IN CERTAIN REGIONS, finding these woods available for purchase might be difficult. They're also rather pricey. Untreated pine is less expensive than treated pine, but it has a shorter lifetime.

ANOTHER FACTOR TO consider is that, with the exception of pine, these woods are not as long-lasting as other materials. These woods are frequently taken from old-growth forests. If you use one of these woods, be sure it's from a sustainable source. Any wood you buy should have the Forest Stewardship Council (FSC) certification. The Forest Stewardship Council (FSC) is an international organization that has created guidelines for sustainable forest management.

AT SOME TIME, all forms of untreated wood will need to be replaced. The sort of wood you use and the environment you live in will determine how long your wood lasts. Untreated wood can endure for several years if you live in a dry area. Untreated timber may only last a couple of years if you reside in a hot and humid climate.

REPLACING your wood does not imply that you have failed. The untreated wood is degrading and, in the process, giving nutrients to your plant bed. It's more of a question of upkeep and determining what would work best for you and your family.

- **Wood Stains and Paint**

YOU MAY STAIN or paint your untreated wood to make it last longer. I suggest utilizing a natural therapy such as raw tung oil or raw linseed oil.

IT'S critical to seek for them in their raw form, as any that aren't tagged "raw" are likely to include additional compounds. Because the chemicals are added to speed up the drying of the oil, utilizing the raw versions allows for more drying time.

ANOTHER CONSIDERATION IS that linseed oil is a mildew food source, so if mildew is a problem in your area, this may not be the best option for you.

THERE HASN'T BEEN much research done on the effects of painting or staining garden beds. The chemicals in paint and stains differ, and the total impact is unclear. However, common sense should warn you that all of these products include chemicals of some sort, and those chemicals may have an influence on your crop.

TREATED wood has been treated with chemical components to help it last longer—the most prevalent type of wood used to be CCA (Chromated Copper Arsenate). The most serious issue with treated wood is that the infused components leak out. Because of the arsenic in CCA, producers of CCA-treated wood stopped making it for domestic use in 2003.

. . .

Although earlier CCA-treated wood may be found, today's retail alternatives are more likely to be ACQ (Ammoniacal Copper Quat) or MCA (Micronized Copper Azole). They have a greater copper content but are devoid of arsenic.

Under the following circumstances, **leaching occurs at the greatest levels:**

- Smaller surfaces, such as the ends and, particularly, sawdust
- More frequently treated (although CCA-treated wood is shown to retain uniformly high levels of CCA)
- Conditions that are wet, such as after a rainstorm or in a humid climate
- In a contaminated environment

To put this in context, research looking at the influence of treated wood in raised beds has found that the most significant danger is actually contacting the bed's outside. When you (or your children) sit on or lean on treated wood, the copper or arsenic seeping out of the wood will most likely enter into your skin or clothing and remain on the surface.

Don't be concerned if your beds are constructed of the older CCA-treated wood. Plants don't even take up arsenic until the soil is low in phosphorus, so you should be OK if you use a lot of compost. Because phosphorus is immobile and continuous compost amendments contribute to the overall amount, this is unlikely to be the case.

. . .

IN OTHER WORDS, good soil with enough organic matter prevents plant roots from absorbing arsenic. However, the more acidic or alkaline your soil is, the more likely your plants are to absorb those elements. So obtaining a soil test is also a good way to move your soil closer to a neutral pH (6.5-7.0, which is also the optimal range for vegetable growth). The same goes for soil with a low organic matter content; therefore, make sure your soil analysis includes an organic matter percentage test.

PLANTS in your food garden won't be able to withstand high amounts of copper in the newer ACQ and MCA treated wood (which have greater copper levels), and studies suggest that good soil also limits copper uptake.

PLANTS WILL PERISH before you have an opportunity to consider eating them, even if copper levels are high and being taken up. That would, in any event, be a good sign of possible concern, and you should consider getting your soil tested for metal concentrations.

WHILE WE'RE on the issue, root vegetables are the most vulnerable to leaching since most metals (once absorbed) stay in plant roots. According to studies, the surface of such root crops is the most impacted. You may eliminate any contamination by carefully rinsing off any affected soil and removing the skin off your potatoes, beets, and other root vegetables.

. . .

THE ROOTS of tomatoes and eggplants may absorb copper and arsenic, but they haven't been demonstrated to damage the fruit. Leafy greens, on the other hand, can absorb arsenic from their leaves.

IN A NUTSHELL, keep your soil near neutral and add plenty of compost (more on these later), carefully wash out the dirt and peel the skin off your root veggies, and prevent touch with the treated wood's exterior surface. Grow leafy greens and root vegetables farther away from the treated wood, closer to the middle of your bed (12" from the perimeter if feasible).

FINALLY, when cutting treated wood beds, make sure you cut in a place where the sawdust can be contained. Wear a dust mask and gloves, and clean up the sawdust as soon as possible. It should not be composted.

- **Cinder or Concrete Blocks**

THE FACT IS that the phrases "cinder blocks" and "concrete blocks" are often used these days interchangeably. Although your "cinder" blocks may be cinder blocks if they are decades old, only concrete blocks have been manufactured for the previous 50 years.

WHAT ARE the materials used to make your concrete blocks? Although it varies depending on your location, there are certain commonalities. Portland cement and aggregate, such as sand or gravel, are used to make almost all concrete blocks.

· · ·

FLY ASH IS one of the components of Portland cement (ranging from 15 percent to 25 percent). It's utilized to produce concrete blocks that are lighter while yet being robust. Fly ash is a refined powder that is produced as a result of coal combustion; therefore, it is a petroleum byproduct.

AND HERE'S THE CATCH: fly ash includes a variety of hazardous elements, including arsenic, lead, and mercury, in varying quantities. Yes, such metals can also be found in the concrete blocks that surround your vegetable garden.

WHILE THIS MAY SOUND ALARMING, the possibility of those metals being released into the earth occurs only if a portion of the concrete block is crushed. A number of criteria then determine the potential risk to what you're cultivating.

THE PROXIMITY of plant roots to the injured region is the first consideration. Finally, greater organic matter soils are usually helpful, especially in this situation, since they assist chemically bind the metals, rendering them inaccessible for uptake by the plant. Root crops and leafy greens, like CCA-treated wood, are particularly vulnerable when exposed to greater quantities.

So, how much fly ash does soil within a concrete block building absorb? If the block is still intact, the chances are little to none. However, there hasn't been much study done on this topic.

. . .

If your beds are built of concrete blocks, stay away from anything that might cause them to break and the dust from pulverized fragments to come into touch with plant roots.

Seal the inside lining with polymer paint (the most practical choice) or line the inner side with PE plastic if you want to "do something." It's up to you to determine if the effort is worthwhile.

The same hazards and precautions apply if raised beds are built on a concrete surface.

It's not a big deal, and there are a lot of other ways you're likely getting unexpected and toxic things into your body that are considerably more dangerous than these blocks.

- **Composite Wood**

Composite wood is created from recyclable resources and may last for many years. When utilized in lengthy sidewalls, some composite materials can buckle. Again, there haven't been many studies done on the usage of composite wood around foodstuffs.

Is there any chemical or element leak from the composite material? It looks to be a safe product for use in the garden, but there isn't enough information to make a firm judgment.

- **Railroad Ties**

CREOSOTE, an oil extracted from coal tar, is used to make railroad ties. The dark, oily substance seeping out the edges of the ties is creosote, which is used as a wood preservative for industrial applications.

RAILROAD TIES ARE a popular choice for raised beds and garden retaining walls because of their strength. At the same time, little research has been done on the impact of utilizing them to enclose food plants.

- **Galvanized Metal**

THERE ISN'T much scientific evidence on the impact of galvanized metal on the utilization of raised beds. I can tell you that galvanizing is usually done by immersing the metal in molten zinc or a zinc-based coating.

ZINC IS a micronutrient that plants and people require in tiny amounts, but it is toxic if taken in high amounts. If too much zinc were leached into the soil, it would most likely manifest itself in dead plants before posing a health concern.

FOR MANY YEARS, galvanized metal has also been used to contain or convey water for people and cattle. To summarize, I cannot guarantee that there will be no negative health consequences, but the risk is unquestionably minimal.

. . .

However, keep in mind that heat and drainage are important considerations. Livestock troughs are a popular choice, but they must have a large number of drainage holes in the bottom. So that you don't drown your plant roots, you'll need a way for the moisture to escape.

Metal will absorb and reflect heat from the sun more than other materials, whether you utilize sheet metal or a trough. As a result, your soil may dry up faster, and vegetation in the path of that reflecting force may suffer as a result. The soil closest to the metal that faces the sun will warm up faster than the remainder of the bed.

Tender plants, such as lettuce, should be planted in the center of the bed, where the soil temperature will stay relatively consistent.

- **Tires**

If you must, do so for little more than a season or two. Tires are made from petroleum. The chemicals in their rubber break down in the heat and dampness, and they end up in your soil. They may be practical, or they may appear to be tacky and amusing. Sure, it keeps a tire out of the dump. However, there are more disadvantages to utilizing tires than advantages.

Tires are prohibited at most landfills for a reason. Your family's food should not be exposed to decomposing tire rubber, just as waste should not be.

. . .

TIRES ARE NOT ALLOWED at most landfills. Your family's food should not be exposed to decomposing tire rubber, just as waste should not be.

- **Pre-Made Kits**

IT DOESN'T GET any easier than purchasing one of the various raised bed kits on the market today. These may be trimmed to various lengths and used with composite wood. Some can be costly, and the materials used to make them vary greatly.

- **Liners**

IF YOU'RE USING any of the materials mentioned above that have the potential to leach, you might want to consider lining the bed with plastic. Yes, this will act as a barrier between your soil and the bed material. However, don't forget about the plastic itself.

THERE ARE SEVERAL POLYMERS AVAILABLE, each with a different level of safety. If you're going to use plastic, make sure it's food-grade polyethylene. This is one of the most food-safe polymers available. Only line the bed's outer perimeter, not the bottom surface. Drainage should not be blocked by plastic.

3

HOW TO BUILD A RAISED BED

Raised beds are a great DIY project for individuals who wish to cultivate their own food. You'll want a few tools as well as some dedicated workers. Here are some step-by-step instructions for making a raised bed garden.

CHOOSE THE IDEAL SPOT.

- If you want to produce veggies, you must have full sun.
- Installation will be a snap thanks to the level ground.
- When not in use, tuck veggie beds aside, so they don't detract from the rest of your garden.

PICK a material for your raised bed.

- The most popular option is untreated rot-resistant wood.
- Railroad ties should be avoided since they have been treated with creosote, which can leach poisons into the soil.

DETERMINE the size and design of your raised bed.

- Make your beds no more than 4 feet broad; this will allow you to reach the middle easily.
- The optimum depth is from 12 to 24 inches.
- Allow at least 18 inches between beds and more if you wish to use a wheelbarrow.

BUILD YOUR RAISED BEDS.

- Galvanized screws (corner posts are optional) or planter wall blocks can be used to anchor wooden beds at the corners and seams.
- You can lay stone or brick beds with or without mortar.
- Are you looking for immediate gratification? Try galvanized stock tanks or quick-to-assemble prefabricated raised beds.

LINE THE BOTTOMS of your raised beds

- Corrugated cardboard or newspaper will keep weeds and grass from growing through.

Soil should be added **to your raised beds.**

- 1 part topsoil, 1 part composted manure, and 1 part sand is a good soil mix for raised beds.
- Bagged soils can be utilized as well.

Plant some vegetables.

- Digging will be easy in the soft ground, and your back will thank you when it's time to harvest.
- Rotate your crops every year if you have more than one bed.

DIY Plans for Raised Garden Beds

A raised bed can fit all of these and much more, including an irrigation system, a spot to sit and relax, ornamental elements to beautify your yard, and hardware cloth below the soil for greater insect control.

You don't even have to put in a lot of effort to create one; some can be put up in only a few hours!

This huge collection of garden ideas and plans includes something for everyone, from simple, beginner-friendly designs to more complex designs that need a lot of skill and provide a greater challenge.

Small Raised Beds (under 4 feet)

2×2 Raised Planter

This 2x2 garden bed is ideal for flowers and herbs, and it will fit in even the tiniest of backyards. You'll need a table saw, miter saw, drill driver, and Kreg Jig to make this planter, but if you're clever, you can make it without them. The pattern is a little more complex than typical garden beds. So, if you're a newbie, be prepared for a steep learning curve.

Materials: Wood
Dimensions: 2'7" x 2'7" x 17"
Difficulty: Medium-Hard

The Herb Wheel Planter

Although this wheel garden planter is 32 inches wide, the amount of planting area provided is significantly less than in a traditional square garden bed. On the other hand, it appears to be anything but ordinary and might be a wonderful (and inexpensive) addition to your backyard.

If you want to try this DIY project, be aware that you'll need more than a dozen different equipment and supplies, ranging from various-sized saws, nail guns, sanders, and Kreg jigs, among other things.

Materials: Wood
Dimensions: 2'8" x 2'5" x 1'
Difficulty: Hard

. . .

Kid-Sized Raised Planter with Legs

Few things in life make a green thumb happier than seeing their child take up gardening. The latter aids kids in being more connected to nature, developing life skills, and improving mental clarity. If your kid has expressed an interest in flora and wildlife, this raised bed could just persuade him to go for it. This DIY project is the perfect size for children. It has adequate room to hold tiny veggies and is also mobile.

Materials: Wood
Dimensions: 3' x 2' x 20"
Difficulty: Easy

Deck Post Herb Planter

If you are a herb lover, you'll love this herb planter. It doesn't take much to make — just an extra day, some basic carpentry skills, and some readily available materials. The raised herb planter is both compact and weather resistant. You'll also have a spot to hang your gardening equipment, thanks to the side hooks. There are no details left out in this guide, and it also includes a printable cut list.

Materials: Wood, deck posts, balusters, plastic utility tub
Dimensions: 3' x 2' x 3'
Difficulty: Medium

Multi-Level Garden Bed

Planting cool-season veggies like beets, broccoli, and cauliflower is one of your favorite things to do. Maybe you're wondering how you might make them last longer in the heat. If so, this multi-leveled garden planter is a must-see. The planter's height not only keeps it safe from wandering animals but also offers shade for cool-season plants on the lower level while enabling summer plants on the upper level to bask in the sun.

Materials: Wood
Dimensions: Vary
Difficulty: Easy-medium

Vertical Garden Pyramid

It's no surprise that vertical gardening is becoming more popular. This approach is simpler to keep up with. Harvesting is simple and typically results in a better harvest. Check out this garden pyramid concept if you want to try vertical planting. When cutting, just keep compound angles in mind. This will need some carpentry abilities, so practice with scrap wood first to avoid wasting your pyramid supplies.

Materials: Wood
Dimensions: 3' x 3' x 6'
Difficulty: Medium-Hard

Reused Masonry Raised Garden

So you've got a lot of new masonry and bricks lying around? Calling a grab hire business to come and collect your garbage is the quickest option, but don't do it just yet!

You'll need a shovel, rake, and a 4' board to start building. Keep in mind how much space you have and which herbs you want to grow. Different herbs require different amounts of room to thrive, and some can be rather invasive.

Materials: Chimney tiles, cinder blocks
Dimensions: 3'4" x 3'4" x 8-12"
Difficulty: Easy

Raised Bed with Built-In Benches

This design is taller than most raised beds, and it includes seats for sitting while harvesting, watering, or planting in your garden. If you have any woodworking expertise, the project will only take you half a day. This raised bed concept is a great present for elderly gardeners or anybody seeking a unique way to dress up their yard.

Materials: Wood
Dimensions: 3'8" x 4' x 18.25" (67.5" x 67.5" w/ benches)
Difficulty: Hard

Medium Raised Beds (4-7 feet)

Elevated Wood Garden Bed

You'll adore this raised bed concept, especially if you live in an apartment, a condo, or somewhere else where an in-ground garden isn't possible. The writers didn't set out to create a decorative object. On the other hand, this garden bed is a great addition to any patio or deck, especially once fresh, organic veggies begin to grow in it. Each bed takes up one square foot, so make more if you need more room for your vegetables.

Materials: Wood
Dimensions: 4'4" x 3'4" x 3'
Difficulty: Medium

Leggy Raised Garden Bed

This mini-raised garden bed might be the answer if your pets are continually causing havoc in your yard or if you have trouble stooping over to weed and water the plants. On the other hand, the arrangement makes water retention difficult.

Materials: Pressure-treated wood
Dimensions: 4' x 4' x 3'
Difficulty: Easy

. . .

Square Foot Grid **Garden Bed**

The square foot gardening technique is used in this raised garden bed design. The concept is straightforward. Create square-foot squares, line them up, and start planting! The technique is an excellent approach to create a tiny yet densely planted garden. This guide will lead you through every step of the process, from selecting a place to preparing adequate soil to the final touches.

Materials: Wood, weed-blocking material
Dimensions: 4' x 4' x 6"
Difficulty: Easy

4×4 **Raised Bed**

This lovely raised bed has plenty of area at the bottom for your vegetables' roots to spread out and gain a stronger hold on the soil. The slats have a little bend for added aesthetic appeal. When unruly pets, toddlers, and other things smash into it, this raised bed can retain its dirt in place and stand its ground. For a splash of color in your landscape, you may also paint the stiles a different color.

Materials: Wood
Dimensions: 4' x 4' x 16"
Difficulty: Medium-Hard

Stylish and Decorative **Raised Bed**

They say, "Simplicity is beauty." However, there's nothing wrong with making your designs a little more complicated! Diamond patterns on these ornamental planters are optional, but they may help bring additional color and diversity to your environment.

Materials: Wood

Dimensions: 4'4" x 4'4" x 12.5"
Difficulty: Medium

Cinder Block Raised Bed

Not everyone is skilled with saws and wooden planks. Maybe you're a gardener who falls into this group. But, surely, you can lift things and arrange them in their proper places? Instead of using wood, this one employs cinder blocks, which eliminates the need to measure, cut, and operate with power equipment. All you have to do now is select the ideal location, level the ground, and set the blocks, and you're ready to start growing your favorite vegetables!

Materials: Cinder blocks
Dimensions: 4'8" x 4'8" x 8"
Difficulty: Easy

The Self-Watering Salad Table

You enjoy the idea of growing your own food and consuming it. But what if tilling and removing sod, as well as making a mess, isn't your cup of tea? If that's the case, consider making your own salad table. The built-in self-watering mechanism wicks water from the container to the roots, lifting your greens and keeping them away from pests on the ground. It requires more upfront effort. However, after you've finished building, it's pretty much set and forget.

Materials: Wood, plastic bins, PVC
Dimensions: 5'3" x 2'3" x 3'
Difficulty: Medium

Cedar Raised Boxes

Building a raised bed vegetable garden may take up a lot of

areas and take up the majority of your yard. While a square is ideal, you may find that you need a mix of square and rectangular beds tucked around the corners to make room for your grass in the center. If this is your situation, this straightforward DIY guide is just what you want.

Materials: Wood
Dimensions: 6' x 3' x 15" or 4' x 4' x 15"
Difficulty: Easy

Cap-Railing Raised Garden Beds

This garden bed design offers enough area for tomatoes and other spreading plants at 3 feet wide and 6 feet long, yet it's still narrow enough to access the middle from either side. The cap railings offer a touch of intricacy, but they also provide the garden bed a more completed aspect and provide a place to rest and store your equipment.

Materials: Wood
Dimensions: 6' x 3' x 2'
Difficulty: Easy-Medium

Keyhole Elevated Garden

Compared to a typical raised garden bed, this arrangement offers a number of advantages. It is built around a composting basket and employs many layers to keep moisture in the soil, resulting in a highly productive garden. Plants are also protected from the intense heat of the sun and the severe winter temperatures by utilizing stone to construct the keyhole/garden bed. This garden bed will need a lot of hard lifting, but it will be well worth the effort.

Materials: Stone, basket material, or branches
Dimensions: 6' circle
Difficulty: Easy

. . .

Cedar Raised Garden Beds

Cedar is a versatile wood that may be used for a variety of projects. It resists decay, insects, and the elements without the use of pesticides, and it's also cost-effective.

Materials: Cedar fence boards
Dimensions: 6'2" x 1'7" x 1'
Difficulty: Easy

Dog-Proof Raised Planter

If you don't have much garden space or only have a balcony, this DIY project may be ideal for you. This elevated planter has a liner made of scrap steel from a roof, drainage holes drilled around the base, and a structure made of heavy-duty wood. Its 2-foot planting depth means you can grow everything from carrots to cucumbers in this sturdy and surprisingly large container. Most importantly, because of its height, it is dog-proof—no digging through the plants here.

Materials: Wood, sheet steel (old roofing), landscaping fabric
Dimensions: 6.25' x 2' x 3'
Difficulty: Easy-medium

Raised Bed With Removable Side Fences

Raised beds help to manage pests and animals to some extent. And the taller the wall is, the better the critter protection. A higher wall, on the other hand, adds to the inconvenience. So, how are you going to get around this issue? Simple. Add moveable partitions. The nicest aspect is that you don't have to start from the beginning. You may include them in your current garden beds.

Materials: Wood, dowels, PVC, furring strips
Dimensions: 8' x 2' x 3'
Difficulty: Easy-Medium

Heavy-Duty Raised Garden Enclosure

Pick up this DIY idea if you have woodworking skills and a whole weekend to spare. It's comparable to the previous garden enclosure, but this one goes a step farther in terms of intricacy and structural integrity. This project will need a large number of supplies and tools.

Materials: Lumber, chicken wire
Dimensions: 8' x 8' x 6'
Difficulty: Hard

Large U-Shaped Raised Bed

This raised bed is rather large, so make sure you have enough room in your home before attempting it. In addition, you'll need at least $500 and a lot of dirt to fill the garden bed. This garden bed isn't for everyone, but it's ideal for people who are serious about producing their own food.

The original idea calls for untreated pine, but go with the tried-and-true cedar if you want to get more bang for your money.

Materials: Wood
Dimensions: 16' x 9' x 2'
Difficulty: Medium-Hard

Railway Sleeper Raised Beds With Benches

Even after they've retired from the train, wooden railway sleepers have a variety of uses. The only limit to how these sturdy pieces of wood may be used is one's creativity. This design transforms railway sleepers into elevated beds, complete with seats.

Materials: Railway sleepers, wood
Dimensions: 21' x 8' x 3'
Difficulty: Hard

Used Tire Raised Bed

If you have any old tires around the house, this guide might be exactly what you need to put those scraps to good use. However, keep in mind that this job will need some serious sawing and the use of power equipment.

Materials: Old tires, cutting tools
Dimensions: Depend on the size of the tire, generally 2-3' round
Difficulty: Medium

U-Shaped Raised Bed

A square garden bed may provide a number of benefits. If building one for your yard isn't an option, this connected raised bed concept may be ideal. It's straightforward to follow, and the materials and tools you'll need are readily available. Cold frames are a great addition to this garden bed if you want to get an early start or prolong the outdoor growing season by a few weeks.

Materials: Wood
Dimensions: Not specified, variable
Difficulty: Easy

Upcycled Pallet Planter

For a variety of reasons, wooden pallets make great planters. They're simple to dismantle and repurpose. They are widely available. If you have to buy them, they are inexpensive, and if you're lucky, you could even receive them for free!

MATERIALS: Old pallet wood
   Dimensions: Variable (depends on pallet size)
   Difficulty: Easy

REPURPOSED **Dresser Herb Garden**

Repurposing is fantastic! Giving old objects a fresh lease on life not only saves you money but also gives you a calming and pleasant sensation. This guide will show you how to prep and transform an old dresser into a new spring garden if you have one that you no longer use. What's more, guess what? You won't even need to disassemble the dresser or make any cuts. You may leave the dresser as is after filling it with soil and plants for an antique look. Alternatively, you may paint it to improve its appearance.

   Materials: Old dresser
   Dimensions: Depend on the size of dresser used
   Difficulty: Easy

INSPIRED NATURAL WOOD **Raised Bed**

Almost all of the guides in this collection involve hardware store items, with the exception of this one. Repurposing is taken to a whole new level in this guide. It's made up of straight wood, thinner branches, and thicker logs that are easy to get by. Before you get started, you'll need to think about a few design considerations. However, the end product will be well worth the effort: a raised garden bed that is as natural as possible.

   Materials: Scrap lumber, old branches
   Dimensions: Variable depending on what you need

Difficulty: Medium

Timber Raised Beds

These timber-raised beds are simple to construct. You'll need a drill, a mallet, hefty screws, and a measuring tape. Plus, because it only takes a day to create, you'll have no trouble fitting it into your schedule.

Materials: Timbers
Dimensions: Variable by personal need
Difficulty: Easy-Medium

Reclaimed Wood Raised Beds

It's really great to work with reclaimed wood. The majority of them have a wonderful patina from age or antique hue from the original paint. Not only that, but it's accessible virtually everywhere. You may begin by taking a look around your home and area. Free recovered wood may be found in abundance in barns, buildings, and old fences.

Materials: Reclaimed wood
Dimensions: Variable depending on wood availability
Difficulty: Easy

Repurposed **Bed Support Raised Bed**

If you utilize your imagination, you can reuse almost everything around you. The creator of this raised bed, for example, changed a bed's base support into a stage for children's play – and then turned it into a raised garden bed when her children outgrown the space. But, even better, her garden bed design includes a structure for vine support. Cucumbers, tomatoes, and peas go well with it.

Materials: Repurposed bed support

Dimensions: Variable – depends on bed
Difficulty: Easy

Willow Wattle Garden Edging For Raised Beds

Ancient Rome used woven stick fences, particularly the wattle kind. This time-honored style of fencing has several advantages. Flexible wooden branches are braided around stakes to create a strong and natural border that can be easily shaped and filled to create a raised bed.

Materials: Willow branches or another flexible greenwood
Dimensions: Variable – depends on need
Difficulty: Easy-Medium

Milk Crate 'Air Pot' Garden

Milk crates offer a lot of versatility and gardening enjoyment. You don't even have to create anything with this! You'll need landscape fabric, scissors, dirt, seedlings, and, of course, milk crates, which are quite simple to find.

Materials: Milk crates, landscaping fabric
Dimensions: Variable depending on the number of crates
Difficulty: Easy

Countertop Raised Beds

People with backaches will appreciate how a high raised bed removes the need to squat and bend over. However, dirt isn't always expensive. How will you fill a large, deep raised garden bed with dirt without breaking the bank?

Materials: Wood, milk crates, hardware cloth, landscaping fabric
Dimensions: Variable – build to suit
Difficulty: Easy

Concrete Vegetable Garden

Why not build a garden bed to suit the present architecture if your backyard has more concrete than soil? You may construct simple concrete blocks from the outside of the bed with finishing blocks on top that are whatever size or form you choose.

Materials: Concrete blocks and toppers
Dimensions: Variable
Difficulty: Easy

7 Common Mistakes in Raised Bed Gardening

Whether you're new to growing your vegetables in a raised bed garden or are a gardening beginner in general, you're bound to make a few errors here and there. There are a few mistakes everyone makes when they're starting out. Mistakes are meant to be learned from, so don't worry. I'll help you learn from some of the most common mistakes before you even get started.

Gardening errors are common even amongst prolific gardeners. Once into a certain habit, it's a bit hard to break that habit. But you can avoid certain common gardening errors with this handy list.

- *Wrong type of plant for your area.*

There are plants for almost all climates, including cooler climates. Some plants are more likely to grow in areas than other plants. Choosing the right plant for your area can be tough. But knowing your area's climate can help.

Ask your local agricultural department for a list of common native plants for your area. You could also ask a local greenhouse or plant nursery for a list.

- *Planting too early.*

SOMETIMES IN EARLY SPRING, the weather might turn warm. This gives gardeners a sense of hope for the start of the gardening season. But this sense of hope can lead to disaster. Some plants tolerate some cooler weather, but some, such as vegetables and some flowers, do not tolerate the cooler weather. As a result, the cooler weather can severely limit production and may even outright kill the plant.

BE careful and know what your gardening zone is. Know the last frost and freeze dates of your area. Most agriculture and local greenhouses departments know these dates and would be more than happy to relay this information to you if you ask.

- *Watering: Too much or too little.*

WATERING IS A VERY important chore in the garden. Plants need water to survive. Too little water and the garden won't grow.

FOR MOST PLANTS, you need about an inch of water a week. Some plants need more; some need less. Usually, vegetables need a little more once they start setting fruit. A trick to find out if you need to water the garden is to stick your finger about two inches into the soil. If it is damp, then you won't have to water. If it is dry, then the garden probably needs water.

Plants need water for survival. But too much water is just as problematic. The water causes the plants to droop. It can also cause germination problems. As a result, the seeds might not grow, or they will grow severely weak stems.

- *Too much fertilizer.*

Some gardeners get zealous when they begin to fertilize plants. They put too much fertilizer on plants, and that can cause problems with growth, especially with vegetables. Most vegetables that have too much fertilizer won't produce more fruit and produce. Instead, they will produce less produce and more foliage.

Read the fertilizer instructions very carefully and research whether the plant you are growing needs extra fertilizer.

- *Not enough sun.*

Light is a very important ingredient in the plant's survival. It needs light to make and process the plant's food. Too little light and the plant can't produce enough food and thus will die.

Some plants need a full eight hours of sun to have a healthy production. But some plants will tolerate shade. But even most shade-tolerant plants need some sun.

- *Spacing.*

SPACING PROBLEMS often occur in gardens. Most of the problems are with too little space between plants. Disease and pests are the main problems with spacing plants too close. Follow the proper spacing guides usually given on the seed packages or plant packages. These are generally carefully researched. Following them can lead to a better, healthier garden.

IF YOU WANT to space plants closer, try a raised bed garden. A raised bed garden is a garden bed that is raised above the ground. It is much like a container on the ground. With a raised bed garden, you have much more control over weeds, control of pests, and control the type of soil you put into the garden. You can usually plant closer in the raised bed garden because of your control over this type of bed.

Mistakes Can Be Corrected

Most garden mistakes can be corrected. Just be aware of the common mistakes, and you can avoid later headaches and heartaches in your garden. Avoiding these mistakes in the first place can give you a healthier and faster-producing garden.

Raised bed garden vegetable choices.

Selecting the right vegetables in the right combination is a mistake you can correct later. Still, if you choose the wrong varieties, your introduction to raised bed gardening may become more difficult.

. . .

LET'S SAY YOU begin with a tougher veggie, like asparagus. Then, a beginner can become discouraged waiting for the two or three years it could finally yield a harvest. Or, you might plant a cool-weather crop like lettuce during the wrong season.

START out with some vegetables that are easier to grow while you learn what works well in your raised bed, **including:**

- Tomatoes
- Basil
- Zucchini
- Bell peppers

MAKE SURE THE options you select aren't just easy to grow but also will be enjoyed by your family. For example, there's no point in growing tomatoes if your children are allergic. Instead, choose the veggies you'll eat the most, and you'll be less likely to lose interest in the varieties your garden holds.

IT'S also important that the options you select will do well in your yard. For example, some vegetables are more susceptible to pests, don't work well in humid locations, or can't withstand fluctuating temperatures throughout the year. So take the weather where you live into consideration.

BEGINNERS MAY even want to start out their first year growing an all-herb garden, with easy-to-grow herbs that you can grow both indoors and out. **The easiest herbs to start with include:**

- Basil
- Thyme
- Mint
- Parsley
- Oregano
- Cilantro

4

PREPARING THE GARDEN BED AREA

Perhaps you are very fortunate and have a raw, flat, gorgeous piece of land just waiting for you to come along and lay down some beds. No? Then you're like the rest of us who have (or have had) to spend some blood, sweat, and tears into reclaiming our garden space from grass, shrubs, and weeds.

If your space is currently lawned:

- Rent a sod cutter to swiftly and simply remove the turf – but be aware that this will come at a cost.
- Sod should be dug up the old-fashioned method.
- That high-maintenance grass should be smothered and composted. This approach will produce a nutrient-rich basis for your garden bed if you are prepared to wait a short time (a few months).

If your space is currently infested:

- Solarizing takes a while (4-8 weeks), but it's a wonderful technique to eliminate weeds and seeds below the soil surface for 2-3 inches. Solarization makes use of stored moisture and heat, and it's best done during the summer's warmest months.
- To solarize, mow the area as low as possible to the ground, then fully water it - really soak it. Then, using clear plastic sheeting, cover the space (clear plastic allows more heat from the sun to penetrate to the soil surface than black or cloudy plastic).
- A good seal of the plastic borders is essential for solarization. Your aim is to keep all of the liquid trapped beneath the surface and prevent heat from escaping. It's preferable to bury the plastic's edges in an inch or two of earth.
- Check the area often during the summer to ensure that the plastic is still well-sealed. If any holes are punched into the plastic during the solarization process, cover them with duct tape.
- At most, don't leave the plastic on for more than eight weeks. Some helpful bacteria in your soil will be killed by solarization, but they will soon repopulate the region. Remember that this procedure kills weeds down to approximately 3" of soil, so digging after solarization will bring those deeper weed seeds back to the surface, causing you additional trouble.
- The eventual removal of plastic sheeting is one disadvantage of solarization. If at all feasible, recycle the plastic.

It isn't critical how your raised beds are oriented. What matters is how your plants are taught.

Bermudagrass:

- If you're up against this foe, solarization is your most effective weapon. Bermuda grass is produced on purpose in some locations, but it may also become a weed that is difficult to eradicate. It has runners that grow above ground and rhizomes that develop below ground.
- Solarization can destroy Bermuda grass runners as well as certain rhizomes, which is excellent news. However, those rhizomes can reach depths of six inches or more, well beyond the reach of solarization heat. So, while solarization can help with Bermuda grass, expect to fight this war for many years to come.
- Because Bermuda grass is so tenacious, it's the only time I'd contemplate putting a layer of landscape fabric behind my raised bed constructions. Alternatively, you may use many layers of cardboard.
- To keep Bermuda grass from creeping in from the perimeter, it is advisable to construct a border around the edge of your bed. Bermuda grass requires a lot of sunshine to grow; therefore, it's less likely to sprout from beneath layers of dirt. Any sprouts in your garden are most likely the result of seeds blown in.

If your space is currently shrubbed:

- A stump or two may need to be ground out or dug out in some situations. On the other hand, raised beds to eliminate the need to remove the majority of the stumps and roots that remain. Much of the leftover woody material will be buried in your garden beds and will eventually decompose, giving nutrients to the soil.

You may also till the garden area to remove existing roots, weeds, and other debris, as well as to level the ground. Tilling can save time and make it simpler to level a surface. Just be aware of the disadvantages before proceeding. Tilling might result in the loss of important soil structure components. As with any of these options, once you've educated yourself on the advantages and disadvantages, you may choose the path that best suits you.

If you're constructing on a hardscape:
Drainage is also a consideration. Water should be able to flow out of the raised bed's bottom onto the concrete. Some people place cardboard beneath the bed frame to aid with water retention, but this isn't a real step because the cardboard would break down so rapidly.

If gravel is your sole option, be aware that it may obstruct drainage. Water does not travel as readily from a dense to a less dense layer, according to studies.

When Should You Plant?

When determining when to plant your garden, there are numerous variables to consider. The first consideration is the sort of plant you intend to use. Some plants, such as lettuce and broccoli, can withstand cold temperatures. Basil and tomatoes, for example, are likely to be harmed or destroyed by temperatures below 40 degrees.

Frost dates and soil temperature are other key variables. The major gardening season in planting zones 3 to 6 occurs between the first and final frost dates. Cold-sensitive plants should not be planted until the threat of frost has gone. Depending on your growth zone, this usually occurs between March and May.

Heat, rather than frost, may decide your planting dates if you cultivate in zones 8-10. Warm-weather gardeners prefer to plant in the fall rather than the spring to avoid the summer heat. Others prepare for two planting seasons every year: early autumn and late winter.

The temperature of the soil is also an important factor to consider while planting. A soil temperature of 60 to 70 degrees F is ideal for most plants. Peas and spinach, for example, germinate well and grow well in good (45 degrees F.) soil. Others, such as eggplant and melons, will not germinate or develop properly unless the soil temperature is over 60 degrees Fahrenheit.

. . .

TOMATOES, peppers, squash, and maize, for example, are generally planted just once every growing season. Salad greens, roots crops, peas, and beans, for example, can be sown and harvested early in the season, then replanted later in the season for a second harvest.

FOLLOWING the planting of the seeds, the area should be properly watered to a depth of several inches. Until the seeds germinate and the young plants have formed their first sets of true leaves, the soil should be maintained constantly wet. Before the seedling within may emerge, the hard covering on most seeds must be loosened for many days. The process will be disrupted if the soil dries up during this period, and you may need to reseed. Covering newly planted areas with garden cloth (or, in the summer, shade netting) keeps the top layer of soil wet. Once the seeds have sprouted, and the plants have established themselves, the cover may be removed.

YOUNG SEEDLINGS SHOULD BE PUT into the garden when the weather is quiet, chilly, and drizzling. If you put tender seedlings on a bright, hot, or windy day, they will suffer. If the weather isn't cooperating, properly water your new seedlings after planting, then cover them with a garden cloth for a few days. Before the plants can take moisture and nutrients from the soil, they must first develop new roots. You may want to find another way to protect them from the sun and to dry the breeze if you don't cover them with a garden cloth. For the first couple of weeks, make sure to water these new plants every day or two.

Tending Your Garden

Weeds are kept to a minimum by planting. You may need to weed a bit every week in the early spring, but by midsummer, your weeding duties should be done. When weeds appear, pull them out as soon as possible, so your vegetable plants don't have to compete for moisture, nutrients, or root space.

IN A RAISED BED, the soil does not dry up as quickly as it does in a typical garden. The bed's edges assist in keeping moisture in the soil, while the plants shade the soil to decrease evaporation. Except in hot weather and droughts, your watering duties should be modest once your plants are well-established.

CROPS THAT TAKE three to four months to mature generally benefit from a second fertilizer treatment in the middle of the season. A monthly dose of water-soluble fertilizer, especially one containing humid acid, seaweed, and fish emulsion, is beneficial to almost all plants. These water-soluble nutrients are quickly absorbed by plants and aid in their health during stressful times. This is a simple approach to reduce insect and disease issues.

AS SOON AS your garden appears to be ready to eat, you may begin harvesting it. At or near the height of maturity, crops are generally the tastiest and most nutritious. Remove any damaged or diseased plant material, as well as any wasted fruit or leaves. Keep an eye out for pests and take care of any problems right away.

. . .

For example, Pole beans and most tomatoes require a cage, trellis, or other support to grow correctly and yield a decent crop. Plant supports also assist in preserving space, keep the garden tidy, and make harvesting plants easier.

To maintain your plants healthily and productive, you'll also need to fertilize them. You'll also need garden cloth (row coverings) for transplanting and frost protection, as well as plant ties and a watering wand or can.

Watering

Mother Nature would deliver an inch of rain every week to keep our crops and flowers completely happy in an ideal world. Because it is unlikely, it is up to us to ensure that our plants receive the water they require to grow.

A rain gauge will assist you in keeping track of the amount of rain that has fallen, but that is just half of the story. The ability of different types of soil to store water varies. Because each tiny particle of clay has a large surface area for water to grasp, a clay-based soil retains water. Because of its larger particles, sandy soil allows water to move through faster. Healthy loamy soil holds some moisture while draining effectively.

Compost increases the soil's capacity to provide precisely the appropriate quantity of water to your plants. Consider sandy soil to be a wire basket full of golf balls: turn on the hose, and the water will flow straight through it. Water still goes through when you add compost, but part of it is held in the sponges. Clay soils benefit from compost because it aerates them and improves drainage. Plants take oxygen through their roots, and if the soil remains wet for weeks at a time, they may drown. This may be avoided with the use of raised beds and compost.

Using your hands is the greatest method to keep track of soil moisture. It should feel somewhat moist when you press your finger into the dirt, like a wrung-out sponge. Get your fingertips down to the root zone (3), not just the surface "at least once a week, deep or so).

Plants may wilt in the heat of the day in hot weather. This isn't necessarily an indicator of a lack of moisture. It's often just a technique for the plant to save moisture by reducing moisture loss via its leaves. Examining the dirt reveals the truth.

Moisture loss is minimized by planting densely in a raised bed garden. Plants provide shade to the soil surface and wind protection to one another.

Mulching around plants with 2-3 inches of mulch "Another efficient approach to retain moisture and provide organic matter to the soil is to use shredded leaves or straw.

There are numerous choices if you conclude that your garden needs water. A watering wand will swiftly send a large amount of water to exactly where you want it. Are you too busy throughout the week to water your plants? Purchase a water timer to turn on a sprinkler or soaker hose automatically. Soaker hoses and drip irrigation systems with emitters are a particularly effective way to get water since they leak water slowly directly at the soil level.

Don't allow the soil to dry up entirely to maintain your plants healthily and fruitful. If the plant's delicate root hairs die, it must focus its energy on regrowing them rather than producing fruit. Plants that are water-stressed can also become bitter and abrasive.

5

GROWING FRUITS AND VEGETABLES IN YOUR RAISED BED GARDEN

There's just something about a well-kept raised bed garden that appeals to me! Everything appears to be new, well-kept, and well-planned. On the other hand, raised beds aren't simply the prettiest method to grow your veggies: they're also a great way to increase production, cope with difficult soil, and keep weeds at bay.

MANY DIFFERENT VEGETABLES may be grown on raised beds, although some are more suited to them than others. Naturally, you'll want to select veggies that your family enjoys.

MAKE sure you plan out how you'll use the space in your raised bed, so you don't run out of room to grow all of the veggies you desire.

20 Simple Veggies That You May Produce in Your Raised Beds:

- *Carrots*

Carrots are simple to grow on a raised bed and are straightforward to sow. A raised bed's loose, aerated soil provides plenty of area for root crops like carrots to thrive. Varied kinds have different requirements, but on a square foot of area, you can plant around 18 carrots. Carrot seeds are quite tiny and only need to be sown 14 inches deep. Water the carrots gently, being careful not to wash away the tiny seeds.

PLANT twice as many seeds as you anticipate growth in your area. You should thin the carrots as they develop to ensure that they have enough area to grow. For a continual crop, succession plant carrots throughout the season.

- *Kale*

EACH PLANT of kale requires around a square foot of area. It also loves cooler temperatures, so put your kale where it will get some afternoon shade. For example, if you have tomato plants in your raised bed, you might put the kale where the tomato plants provide shade in the afternoon.

PLANT KALE PLANTS approximately a foot apart in the raised bed if you're transplanting them. You can scatter a few seeds in the center of each square foot if you're starting with seeds. When the kale starts to develop, pluck out the weaker seedlings that are growing slowly.

- *Cucumbers*

Cucumbers are available in bush and vine types. You can plant either one in a raised bed, but if your bed is tiny and you want to produce vining cucumbers, you should use a trellis.

Cucumbers trained to climb the trellis will produce fruit that is easy to detect and pluck. Cucumber seeds should be spaced six inches apart and sown no deeper than one inch. If you're using a trellis, place them near to it. You don't have to put them in hills if you don't want to.

- *Lettuce*

Lettuce is a great addition to any raised bed garden. Although it is a cool-weather crop, it grows fast. You may sow lettuce seeds near tomatoes, peppers, and other bigger plants.

Before the bigger plants reach maturity, the lettuce will be ready to pick. You may even cram a few lettuce plants into nooks and crannies.

Cover your lettuce seeds with dirt in a narrow line or a tiny block. They should only be lightly watered to avoid the small seeds being washed away. You may pick lettuce from every other plant once it has established itself, thinning the lettuce as it develops.

WHEN YOU HAVE a little room in your raised bed, continue to sow four-season lettuce seeds every two weeks. This will keep you in fresh greens all summer without taking up a valuable raised bed area.

- *Radishes*

RADISHES ARE one of the fastest-growing vegetables, making them ideal for raised-bed gardening. Radish seeds can be planted with bigger plants.

THE RADISHES WILL BE ready to harvest in 35 to 60 days, well ahead of the maturity of your bigger plants. Radishes may be squeezed into any little gap or area that needs to be filled. Dig a shallow trench where you want your radishes to grow, then scatter the seeds in carefully. Lightly cover them with dirt and water them carefully. Radish seeds are readily wiped away. You may need to thin your seeds if you sow them densely.

- *Spinach*

SPINACH MAY BE GROWN next to lettuce and radishes without causing any issues. It does, however, grow best in colder conditions, so start your spinach early. After it's been picked, put something else there, like radishes, and then plant more spinach in late summer or early fall when the temperature starts to calm down.

. . .

Spinach will germinate in a week if the conditions are correct. Plant it in the same manner as lettuce. You may make a little trench and scatter your spinach seeds along with it. Lightly cover with dirt, then water carefully.

Because spinach may be eaten at any stage, you can collect the young leaves instead of trimming them. Harvest all of the other plants to give the others room to flourish.

- *Tomatoes*

Tomatoes are versatile and simple to produce vegetables. If your raised bed is tiny, you might want to go with a smaller tomato type, such as a cherry tomato. Indeterminate tomatoes will take up more area, whereas determinate tomatoes will take up less.

You may train them to grow on trellises or cages or simply let them droop over the side of your raised bed. Planting starting plants from a nursery is the most convenient option. To allow them plenty of room to grow, space them approximately two feet apart.

- *Cucamelons*

Cucamelons are a good option if you like cucumbers but don't have much room. They resemble small watermelons, but they have a pleasant, lemony cucumber flavor. Because these fragile vegetables grow fast on thin vines, you'll need a trellis to support them.

CUCAMELONS MAY BE STARTED inside in biodegradable pots six weeks before the latest frost date. Allow them to harden off for a week or two before planting the entire container in your raised bed. Using biodegradable containers can help your cucamelons get a head start and reduce transplant shock.

- *Summer Squash*

SUMMER SQUASHES ARE abundant and come in a variety of forms and sizes. Bush types like bush zucchini, yellow squash, and pattypan are good choices if your area is limited. Please provide some breathing space around each plant to allow for adequate air circulation. Otherwise, your plants will be more prone to issues like downy mildew when the weather becomes humid.

THE IMPORTANT ASPECT of these squashes is that they generate a large amount of food in a short amount of time. If you have a trellis or additional space, you may plant vining squash types like spaghetti squash, acorn squash, or even tiny pumpkins.

GROWING A LARGER or heavier type of squash, on the other hand, may need supporting the fruit as it grows. You may achieve this by making a tiny hammock out of old stockings or pantyhose to provide extra support for your squash.

- *Mint*

Mint is a great plant for a raised bed since it can quickly take over a garden or yard. Plant it in a sunny location and frequently harvest after it's established. Just make sure it doesn't take over your whole raised bed! Mint is difficult to cultivate from seed. The easiest approach to cultivate healthy mint is to borrow some from a friend or neighbor who lives in an area with comparable growth conditions and soil.

If feasible, dig up a square foot of roots, being careful to collect lots of them. Plant it in its new location and give it plenty of water. It is drought-resistant and requires minimal care once established.

- *Peas*

Peas are an excellent choice for raised beds since they may produce in as little as 45 days. If you don't have a trellis, use a smaller variety or let the pea vines trail over the edges of your raised bed.

Sow pea seeds early in the season when the weather is still nice. They'll be one of the first plants you may plant in the garden, and they'll be one of the first to produce. They can be planted near together. Harvesting them frequently will encourage plants to produce more.

- *Beans*

You can produce two different varieties of beans on your raised beds. Bush beans are smaller and do not require trellis support. Throughout the summer, succession plants your bush beans every two weeks or so for the optimum crop. Pole beans may also be planted in your raised bed, but they will need to be supported by a trellis, pole, or wire. They will be able to produce beans for a longer period of time.

Plant your beans approximately one inch deep and six or seven inches apart in a sunny area. Bush beans will need to be thinned a little, but pole beans will have plenty of room to climb their trellis. You may use your trellis to provide cool-weather plants like lettuce and spinach with some afternoon shade.

- *Celery*

Celery has a shallow root system, making it perfect for growing on a raised bed. You may grow them from seed, starting plants, or even the heart of a bunch of celery you bought at the store. Celery grows best in colder temperatures, so start your seeds eight to ten weeks before the last frost date. Before putting your seedlings in your raised bed, harden them off.

Celery grows best with lots of water and compost, but don't let it linger in damp soil, or the roots will rot. Once the plant is established, you can continue to harvest from it. To ensure that it continues to grow properly throughout the season, you may wish to side-dress it with some additional compost.

. . .

CELERY MAY BE HARVESTED in as little as 80 days, depending on the variety.

- *Onions*

ONIONS ARE a fantastic choice if you want to cram a few additional veggies into your raised beds. You'll want to keep them away from your peas and beans, though.

BUYING onion sets and planting the small bulbs in early spring is the easiest way to cultivate onions. To give onions a head start on the growing season, start them from seed indoors 8 to 10 weeks before your last frost date. Some vegetables, such as kale, broccoli, cabbage, tomatoes, lettuce, and peppers, maybe naturally insect deterrents, so squeeze your onions in around them.

YOU CAN PUT a few extra onions in the gaps between your larger plants because onions don't take up much room. You may also plant your onions in a block or square foot portion if you like.

- *Peppers*

PEPPERS THRIVE in the sun and heat and can be grown alongside tomato plants if desired. They are simple to cultivate and require minimal upkeep. If you're starting your peppers from seed, start them 8 to 10 weeks before your last frost date indoors.

. . .

PEPPERS, especially chili peppers, can be difficult to cultivate from seed. If you buy starting plants from a nursery, though, you may place them in your raised bed once the threat of frost has gone.

PLANT PEPPER PLANTS 12 to 18 inches apart on average. When the fruit grows heavy, you may want to stake your peppers to give them a little additional support, especially if you're growing bell peppers. Pinch off the blossoms if the plants start to set flowers when they are young to give the plant time to grow before putting its energy into producing fruit.

- *Beets*

BEETS MATURE QUICKLY and can be eaten in as little as 60 days. They do require some room, so place your seeds two to three inches apart and no deeper than an inch. For your beets to grow big enough, make sure your raised bed is at least 12 inches deep.

BEETS MUST BE WELL-WATERED and not allowed to languish in damp soil. Harvest your beets when they're still tiny for a sweeter, tastier result.

- *Potatoes*

THREE TO FIVE pounds of potatoes should be produced by each potato plant. Start with a half-filled potato bed and plant your seed potatoes three inches deep and one foot apart for the greatest results.

. . .

Add dirt or mulch to your raised bed as the potato plants develop. Early potato varieties can be planted closer together, while later varieties will require more space. Make sure you know the potato type you're planting, and when they'll be ready to harvest so you know when to dig them up.

Cucumbers, squash, carrots, turnips, and brassicas do not grow well near potatoes. If you have the space, try giving your potatoes their own raised bed.

- *Arugula*

In a raised bed, this peppery salad green is simple to cultivate. It loves somewhat colder conditions, just like spinach and lettuce. Plant it so that it gets some afternoon shade during the hot summer months. Arugula seeds are extremely small and often misplaced during the planting procedure. Plan out a little area to grow your arugula in for the greatest results.

Make sure the dirt is nice and smooth before scattering the small seeds equally over the top. Pat them in with your hand, then softly water them. Arugula may be harvested when it is young for a sweeter flavor. Plants that are more mature will be spicier. Plants that thrive in the hot summer sun may become bitter and bolt, yet the blossoms are delicious.

- *Swiss Chard*

SWISS CHARD THRIVES in raised beds and container gardens because it is both colorful and healthy. While the weather is still warm, you may start growing Swiss Chard early in the spring. It can withstand both cold and heat with ease.

SET your Swiss Chard at a distance of 12 to 18 inches apart. Make sure it gets enough water. When the leaves are large enough, you can eat Swiss Chard. Younger leaves offer a greater taste and are more delicate.

- *Zucchini*

ZUCCHINI THRIVES under direct sunlight and hot temperatures. As soon as the soil is warm enough, you may straight-sow your zucchini plants into your raised bed or container. To keep the soil aerated and loose, add a lot of old compost. Plant seeds three to four inches apart and half an inch deep. You'll probably need to thin the plants to at least six inches apart once they've established themselves. To avoid blossom end rot, water your plants evenly.

BUSH VARIETIES WILL TAKE up less area in your raised bed, but vining varieties, when planted on a trellis, can make use of vertical space. You can fit a few more plants in if you pick vining kinds. You may even let the vines flow over the sides of your raised beds if you like.

6
MAINTAINING HEALTHY SOIL AND BENEFITS

Though some gardeners are lucky enough to have perfect soil, most of us have to make do with less than ideal soil. Don't despair if your soil contains too much clay, is too sandy, stony, or acidic. Once you grasp the components of good soil, it's not difficult to transform bad soil into plant-friendly soil.

WEATHERED ROCK AND ORGANIC MATERIALS, as well as water and air, make up soil. Small animals, worms, insects, and microbes thrive when the other soil components are in balance constitute the "magic" in good soil.

MINERALS. Approximately half of the soil in your garden is made up of small pieces of weathered rock that have been progressively broken down by the wind, rain, freezing, and thawing, as well as other chemical and biological processes.

. . .

GARDENERS WHO GROW vegetables recognize the value of good soil. The size of these inorganic soil particles is used to classify soil types: sand (big particles), silt (medium-sized particles), or clay (small particles) (tiny particles). The mix of sand, mud and clay particles in your soil defines its texture and impacts drainage and nutrient availability, which affects how effectively your plants develop.

ORGANIC MATTER. The partially decomposed remnants of soil creatures and plant life, such as lichens and mosses, grasses and leaves, trees, and all other forms of vegetative matter, are referred to as organic matter.

ORGANIC MATTER IS VITAL, even though it only makes up a tiny percentage of the soil (typically 5 to 10%). It binds soil particles together, forming porous crumbs or granules that enable air and water to pass through. Organic matter may also absorb and store nutrients while retaining moisture (humus can contain up to 90% of its weight in water). Above all, organic matter provides food for bacteria and other soil life.

COMPOST, aged animal manures, green manures (cover crops), mulches, and peat moss can all help to enhance the quantity of organic matter in your soil. Concentrate on the top 6 inches of soil since it contains the majority of soil life and plant roots.

IF YOU'RE GOING to use a lot of high-carbon material, be careful (straw, leaves, wood chips, and sawdust). In their efforts to digest these items, soil microbes will use a lot of nitrogen, depriving your plants of nitrogen in the near term.

SOIL LIFE. Bacteria and fungus, protozoa and nematodes, mites, springtails, earthworms, and other small animals present in good soil are all examples of soil organisms. These creatures are required for the development of plants. They aid in the conversion of organic materials and soil minerals into vitamins, hormones, disease-fighting chemicals, and nutrients required by plants.

THEIR EXCRETIONS also aid in the formation of tiny aggregates that keep the soil loose and crumbly. It's your responsibility as a gardener to establish perfect circumstances for these soil creatures to accomplish their jobs. This entails providing them with a plentiful supply of food (carbohydrates found in organic matter), oxygen (found in a well-aerated soil), and water (an adequate but not excessive amount).

AIR. About 25% of healthy soil is air. This much air is required for insects, bacteria, earthworms, and soil life to survive. The atmosphere in the soil also serves as a vital supply of atmospheric nitrogen for plants.

PORE SPACE between soil particles or crumbs is abundant in well-aerated soil. Fine soil particles (clay or silt) contain very small gaps between them, often too small for air to get through. Huge-particle soil, such as sand, has large pore spaces and holds a lot of air. However, too much air can hasten the decomposition of organic materials.

ADD LOTS OF ORGANIC MATTER, avoid treading on the growth beds or compacting the ground with heavy equipment, and never work the soil while it's extremely wet to guarantee a balanced supply of air in your soil.

WATER. Water will make up approximately a quarter of healthy soil. Water, like air, is retained between soil particles in the pore spaces. Rain and irrigation water can flow down to the root zone and subsoil through large pore spaces. In sandy soils, the gaps between the soil particles are so wide that water drains down and out relatively fast due to gravity. It's for this reason why sandy soils dry out so quickly.

WATER CAN MOVE BACK UP by capillary action because of the small pore spaces. Water has filled the pore spaces of water-logged soils, pushing all of the air out. Plant roots and soil organisms are both suffocated as a result of this.

YOUR SOIL SHOULD IDEALLY CONTAIN a mix of big and tiny pore spaces. Again, organic matter is crucial because it promotes aggregation or the formation of crumbs or soil. Organic matter absorbs and stores water until plant roots want it.

THESE FIVE BASIC components are found in various proportions in each soil. You may drastically enhance the health of your soil and the output of your garden by balancing them. But first, you must determine the type of soil you have.

. . .

If you keep it in good shape, you won't have to replenish your raised bed soil every few years. You don't need to replenish your raised bed dirt unless your plants bring in a soil-borne illness; otherwise, keep it up! And how can you maintain the soil in raised beds healthy?

Here are some tips:

- *Add compost to your raised bed.*

Compost isn't for preparing spring beds! In the fall, add compost to your raised beds. Compost is a fantastic method to finish the gardening season in raised beds. This compost does not need to be totally broken down because it will sit on the bed all winter. Composting can take place in the raised bed.

Aside from that, it's a fantastic method to get rid of fall yard debris. Cover the bed with a couple of inches of compost and then mulch. The mulch will retain the nutrients in the raised bed while protecting the soil from harsh winter weather.

- *In raised beds, use soil amendments*

In raised beds, soil additives are blended with the soil to enhance the soil quality. What sort of soil amendment you use will determine what effect it has on the soil.

You could wish to use soil amendments to enhance the nutrients in the soil or modify the soil's physical structure, which is referred to as tilth. Simply defined, it's the soil's texture.

. . .

Assume that the soil in your raised bed is drying out too quickly. Perhaps you didn't use the proper soil combination, to begin with. It's possible that your soil included too much sand, causing water to flow fast through the soil before the plants could absorb it.

You may improve the soil by adding organic matter-rich soil amendments, such as compost. The organic matter in the soil will help to keep moisture in the soil. On the other hand, if there is too much water in the soil, you can add greensand to assist water drain more efficiently.

Vermiculite, worm castings, compost, coir, greensand, grass clippings, cornmeal, alfalfa meal, lava sand, straw, and kelp meal are some organic soil additions to consider for improving the quality of your raised bed soil.

- *Plant a crop to serve as a cover crop*

Don't forget about cover crops when it comes to replenishing nutrients in raised beds. Cover crops aren't simply for large-scale farmers that want to keep weeds at bay. They will also help backyard gardeners who use raised beds.

Cover crops aerate the soil, especially if you grow a cover crop like alfalfa, which has a deep root structure. Till the cover crop into the soil a few weeks before planting time. The root system will bring nutrients deep in the soil to the surface, making nutrients easily available when it comes time to plant. This raises organic matter, which improves soil health and nutrient levels.

Consider growing legumes as a cover crop if you want to provide nitrogen to the soil. Alfalfa, fava beans, and red clover are examples of legume cover crops. After the growing season is done, consider winter cover crops to preserve and aerate your raised bed soil while also providing additional nutrients.

- *Gardening with Lasagna*

Another wonderful method for improving soil conditions is lasagna gardening, often known as No-Till gardening or sheet composting. It's also a great way to make a raised bed. You can enhance your soil conditions from the outset, whether you're starting from scratch or working on an existing raised bed garden. As the soil in your raised bed depletes over time, you add layers via sheet composting, just as in a lasagna garden, to thoroughly renew your soil from the top down.

Keep in mind that if you use this approach to repair your raised bed soil, it will take at least six months for the layers to break down before you can plant.

If you're alternating beds or just have one garden season, this approach is ideal. However, if you want to get started sooner, this resource from the link above is a wonderful place to start. If you intend to plant right away, sprinkle two or three inches of compost or dirt on top of the bed and plant directly into it. Then you may get started right now!

- *Prepare for the winter with raised beds*

DON'T FORGET that the conclusion of the gardening season is an ideal opportunity to do a few easy soil management tasks. It's akin to closing up shop for the season. That is unless you live in a climate where you can grow year-round.

HERE ARE two helpful hints **for winterizing your raised beds:**

- *The roots should be left alone.* Don't pull the plant out! Simply cut the plant just above the soil's surface.
- *Decomposition and aeration of the soil will occur when the seeds disintegrate.* Cover the bed with mulch after spreading a few inches of compost over the bed. The mulch protects the soil from the elements over the winter, while the compost adds nutrients. (Alternatively, you can plant a cover crop instead of composting and mulching.)

INSTEAD OF TAKING away the dirt from your raised bed and replacing it with fresh soil, try these five techniques for improving soil quality in a raised bed and save yourself the bother. It's a lot less work than getting rid of everything you have and beginning again. It's also quite good for improving the quality of your soil.

7

PLANTING RAISED BED VEGETABLE GARDENS

Before you start digging, keep in mind which way the light is shining—you don't want your taller plants shading out anything behind them. If you don't read the seed packaging before planting flowers in your raised beds, they may not grow to the desired height. Make sure the heat-loving fruits and vegetables you plant—tomatoes, melons, cucumbers, squash, and so on—get at least six to eight hours of direct sunshine each day (preferably closer to eight).

IF YOU'RE PLANTING seedlings or sowing seeds, read the seed packet or grow tag carefully to find out what circumstances the plants require to thrive. For example, when sowing root vegetables, you'll want to follow the thinning instructions after the sprouts start poking through the dirt. Beet sprouts, for example, maybe preserved and thrown in a salad, even if it seems like a waste when you're plucking them out. On the other hand, carrot seedlings should be buried. Beets, carrots, radishes, turnips, and other root vegetables should be thinned to stimulate healthy root growth and the production of more large crops.

You should give some plants, such as tomatoes, adequate space so that air may move between them—this aids in illness prevention. The light should also be able to reach the plants and fruit. You don't want to position tomatoes too widely apart, either, since this will allow weeds to grow in. Other nightshade vegetables to keep in mind include peppers, eggplant, and tomatillos.

Make a habit of watering your plants on a regular basis, and don't forget to hydrate your fragile young plants. To protect them from a late-spring frost, use cloches or row covers.

Why do you want to plant your raised beds so densely?

Intensive planting is a strategy for reducing the amount of space in the garden where weeds can thrive. When seedlings are planted closer together, the plants themselves function as a live mulch, keeping the soil cool and minimizing evaporation.

Raised bed succession planting

This leads us to the topic of succession planting. There's no reason why you can't add more vegetables to that space if you're taking out your spring harvests like peas and root veggies or your garlic harvest in the summer. Under your grow lights, you might wish to give seedlings a head start. Remember the compost advice while planting: modify the soil to give nutrients and encourage a healthy yield. Healthy soil is essential for a successful garden.

. . .

CHECK the days till your garden crops are ready. After a huge vining plant has ceased producing, you may sometimes be inventive and smuggle in other veggies that mature faster or nestle in a succession crop. Plant and collect radishes, and lettuce greens before bigger plants with swooping tendrils take over the space. Pull big crops like tomatoes, squash, and eggplant after they stop producing and replace them with later-season crops like broccoli, lettuce, and kale, which flourish in the lower fall weather. Before planting the following crop, make sure the soil is amended with organic matter.

MAKE a place for more plants by adding plant supports.
   Give your plants something to climb while you're planting a raised bed—trellises, an old piece of lattice, cattle panels, etc. If you've ever put a squash seedling in a raised bed, you know that the plant will quickly take over half of the garden, if not the entire garden! Cucumbers, squash, beans, peas, and melons will benefit from the addition of vertical structures.

IN YOUR RAISED BEDS, plant a variety of vegetables and flowers.
   Planting food in your decorative gardens and vice versa has several advantages. In your raised beds, you might choose to plant flowers like zinnias, nasturtiums, and cosmos. They attract pollinators, who will pollinate your tomato flowers, squash blossoms, and cucumber blooms (a win-win situation!). Hummingbirds flutter around you in the garden on a hot summer day, seeking zinnias to feed on. Plant a few extra blooms so that you may leave some for pollinators and use the rest to make vases full of summer bouquets.

. . .

When establishing a raised bed, you may also utilize flowers as natural pest control. Some of your plants can be based on pests that have infested your garden in past seasons, while others can be used as preventative measures. Listed below **are a few examples:**

- Alyssum attracts parasitic wasps that eat cabbage worms, cucumber beetles, squash vine borers, tomato hornworms, cutworms, gypsy moth caterpillars, and other undesirable insects.
- Hyssop attracts the two-spotted stink bug, which feeds on the Colorado potato beetle larvae, a pest that wreaks havoc on my tomatillos.
- Marigolds are used to protect soil against nematodes.
- Nasturtiums can be utilized as an aphid trap crop if you don't mind sacrificing a few.

Companion Planting **in Raised Beds**

Companion planting is a great way to boost the production of your veggies while you're planting and growing them in raised beds. A good companion plant will enhance soil nutrient levels, prevent pests, attract helpful pollinators, improve plant flavor, or attract predatory insects that wish to eat on your vegetables for almost every vegetable you produce. When it comes to planting and producing veggies in raised beds, these are some of our favorite combinations.

- To keep the carrot fly at bay, plant onions alongside them.

- To increase the flavor of tomatoes and peppers while also repelling aphids and spider mites, plant basil among them.
- To keep nematodes at bay, plant marigolds near tomatoes.
- Corn and beans should be planted together. Corn is a high-nitrogen feeder, and beans return nitrogen to the soil as they develop. Beans can also use corn as a vertical support system for their vines.
- To prevent the cucumber beetle and aphids, plant marigolds and nasturtiums near cucumbers.
- Heat-resistant carrots and broccoli should be planted in the shadow of taller tomato plants.

THERE ARE many more duos in vegetable gardens that are excellent to grow together, and some plants do not get along—the process of figuring out what works and what doesn't might be aided through trial and error.

PLANTING AND PRODUCING vegetables on raised garden beds is a great idea. They not only make for neat and attractive growing environments, but they may also aid with problems like weeds and pests. Growing vegetables on raised beds and using certain expert planting and growth methods will help you make the most of every square inch of your growing area and increase your garden output dramatically.

8

DEALING AND MANAGING INSECT AND MITE PESTS IN VEGETABLE RAISED BED GARDENS

Insect-infested gardens may be quite healthy and prolific. On the other hand, insect pests can diminish the amount and quality of a vegetable crop and spread illnesses from one plant to another. Control measures may be required if this occurs. When dealing with insects in the garden, ascertain if they are useful or pests by identifying the species. Recognize the most frequent insects in the region, as well as common pests and indicators of pest damage. At least once a week, check the garden for pests.

INSECT PESTS CAN TAKE up a permanent home in the garden, whether they come on foot or by plane. Flying insects are extremely mobile and have the ability to move in big groups. Aphids and mites, for example, may complete their life cycle in approximately a week under ideal conditions, allowing their populations to grow quickly. When a large number of pests emerge overnight, they have either flown in or are quickly multiplying.

. . .

METAMORPHOSIS IS the process through which insects change size, shape, and color as they mature. Plants are harmed by both the juvenile and adult stages of several bug species. Insects can be difficult to recognize since their shapes fluctuate, and their harm to plants also changes. Small caterpillars may just scratch the surface of a leaf, but bigger caterpillars may consume huge pieces.

THE MOUTHPARTS of the insect cause plant damage. Insects with sucking mouthparts eat leaves or fruit, leaving pockmarks or mottled leaves in their wake. Plant tissues are chewed by insects having chewing mouthparts. Knowing how an insect feeds might help a gardener choose the right insecticide; for chewing insects, consider stomach poisons, and for sucking insects, choose contact poisons.

PREPARE AHEAD OF TIME.

Consider potential pests and how to handle them before they cause issues when developing a vegetable garden. To cope with pest problems, implement the management strategy ahead of time.

INTEGRATED PEST MANAGEMENT.

Integrated pest management, or IPM, is a set of pest-control strategies that aim to strike a balance between economic output and environmental care. Today, IPM is the overarching approach for most productive agriculture, and it is also being used in urban areas.

. . .

IPM REQUIRES constant monitoring of crops for the presence and absence of pests. Management is appropriate in circumstances where a pest is present and might cause considerable damage.

INSECTICIDES ARE A CONTROL ALTERNATIVE, despite numerous techniques being applied as part of an IPM program. The IPM technique is similar to organic gardening when non-chemical control practices are utilized.

MANY CONTROL TECHNIQUES are **available for home vegetable gardeners in the areas below:**

CULTURAL CONTROL

Cultural control refers to gardening methods that minimize insect populations or effects. Variety selection, crop rotation, cultivation, weed management, water management, and fertilizer usage are all examples of these techniques. For certain pests, keeping the land fallow and weed-free for a period of time or rotating crops is the best option. Plant waste may serve as a breeding ground for pests, so keep it out of the garden. Weeds can attract insect pests; therefore, they must be kept under control.

HOST PLANT RESISTANCE

Vegetable types can continue to produce despite insects and other pests because of a natural mechanism known as host plant resistance (HPR). Tolerance, non-preference, or antibiosis are all characteristics of these plants. Tolerance refers to a plant's capacity to grow and thrive in the face of insect damage.

When a plant contains features that drive insects to pick other plants, such as plant hairs, repellant smells, or colors, this is known as non-preference. Antibiosis is the production of compounds by some plants that kill or delay the growth of pests.

To FULLY COMPREHEND vegetable host plant resistance, many experiments are required. The majority of variety selections prioritize beauty, flavor, and yield volume over pests. Many cultivars have not yet been evaluated for host plant resistance.

TRANSGENIC PLANTS ARE plants that have had their genetic material changed by researchers, such as tomatoes, potatoes, and maize. When insect resistance genes are introduced into new kinds, dramatic effects can be attained. The genes of the bacteria Bacillus thuringiensis are found in most insect-resistant transgenic crop types, making them immune to certain caterpillar pests. Caterpillars that feed on these plants are hampered by this resistance. Homeowners may expect to see more resistant transgenic vegetable types on the market.

Biological control

Biological control is a method of controlling another organism by using one organism to control another. Importation, conservation, and augmentation are three successful biological control strategies.

IMPORTING a parasite or predator from another nation to manage an invasive exotic pest species is known as importation. Importation is not available to home vegetable growers since it is heavily regulated by state and federal authorities, despite the fact that they profit from successful importation research projects.

NATURAL ENEMIES already present in the region are encouraged by conservation efforts. **The following are some examples of conservation techniques:**

- Planting flowers that produce nectar and offer food for parasites.
- Avoiding the use of pesticides that aren't essential.
- Pesticides that are harmful to pests yet generally harmless to beneficial insects are chosen.

ADDITIONAL PREDATORS AND PARASITES, such as lady beetles, praying mantids, and parasitic wasps, are released into natural populations as a result of augmentation. However, because many of these predators and parasites are already present in the ecosystem, the advantage of additional releases may be negligible.

BIOLOGICAL MANAGEMENT ISN'T a quick fix for insect issues. A thorough investigation is required to support a good biological management program, which must begin with the accurate identification of pests and beneficial species. Increased surveillance is required. Many biological pest management products are only effective against certain insect species. Biological controls are seldom accessible for a specific pest.

. . .

Mechanical control

Barriers, covers, high-pressure water sprays, and hand-picking pests are examples of mechanical control methods that employ physical techniques to minimize bug populations or damage.

Pests are deterred from entering plants by using barriers such as cardboard or plastic cylinders at the base of transplants or fabric or plastic screening to protect a freshly planted garden. An added benefit of screening is that it can raise the temperature of a planting bed. Screening is particularly beneficial for vulnerable young plants and seedlings, and it may also give some frost protection.

When it comes to little, soft-bodied pests like aphids, high-pressure water spraying is one of the few alternatives available when vegetables are nearing harvest. High-pressure water sprays may aid in the removal of webbing, the dissolution of droppings, and the reduction of pest numbers in a short period of time. On the other hand, water sprays may not kill all pests and may spread bugs to other hosts.

In small gardens, hand-picking and killing some pests may be possible, and it can be effective for tomato hornworms and even squash bugs if done consistently. For larger insects, hand-picking is a better option than for tiny ones.

Chemical control

The Environmental Protection Agency (EPA) oversees the sale, and use of pesticides in all forms, and the Texas Department of Agriculture supervises the sale and use of these goods. In the registration procedure, these agencies do not evaluate efficacy. Insecticides with labels may or may not be successful in killing the pests listed on the label. The large variety of goods available for use in home vegetable gardens, as well as the fast turnover in the market, make determining product efficacy difficult. As pests become more resistant or as environmental variables interact with a pesticide, its efficacy might alter. Furthermore, if a pesticide is not used as directed on the label, it may fail.

Less toxic approaches

Many gardeners prefer to employ less harmful pest management methods, ranging from "soft" insecticides to natural control, rather than using traditional chemicals. There are more of these items available to home gardeners than ever before. In pesticide formulations, inert chemicals are frequently used to dilute the active components and make application easier.

Putting *Everything Into Action*
Plant a little garden that will be easy to maintain.
The size of the garden has a direct impact on the feasibility of control methods. In larger gardens, removing pests by hand and swabbing bugs with alcohol may not be possible. Non-pesticidal treatments are less likely to be practical as the garden grows larger.

Before planting, **leave the garden fallow for a while.**
White grubs, wireworms, and cutworms are insect pests that overwinter in the soil and feed on abandoned plants or

weeds. Pest populations are reduced before spring planting by removing these feeding sources during the off-season.

Maintain a clean environment.

Cutworms, slugs, snails, pillbugs, and sowbugs may all gather in dead leaf heaps, boards, railroad ties, and other items. Mulches aid in moisture retention and provide cover for spiders and predatory insects, but they also give pest protection.

Pest-free transplants should be chosen.

Before you buy a plant, inspect it to make sure it's free of pests. The undersides of leaves are home to the majority of insect and mite infestations. Only buy pest-free, healthy transplants.

Choose pest-resistant vegetable cultivars.

Some vegetable cultivars are unappealing or resistant to pests. Insecticide use can be drastically reduced by planting insecticide-resistant cultivars that are tailored to your location. For example, the sweet corn variety "Seneca Sentry" is resistant to corn earworms and well-suited to Central Texas. The leaves that wrap around the corn ear tip are considerably tighter around the silk in more sensitive types. Unfortunately, only a few vegetable types have been tested for pest resistance.

Use proper horticulture techniques.

Before planting, properly prepare the soil until it is free of insects and offers ideal growing conditions for seedlings and transplants. Pests will be less likely to harm healthy plants. Pest populations are also influenced by soil type and spring growth conditions. Even though rich organic matter soils may encourage greater plant development, they are more likely to sustain white grubs, root maggots, pillbugs, and sowbugs.

- **Keep your garden weed-free.** Weeds provide food for insect pests and compete with vegetable plants for soil nutrients and water, resulting in a significant reduction in vegetable output. Grasshoppers and armyworms will be discouraged by a weed-free garden and grass kept short surrounding the garden.
- **Fertilize your garden appropriately.** Plants require sufficient nutrients to thrive. On the other hand, using too much fertilizer might result in lush, green plants that attract aphids and other insect pests. A soil test will reveal which nutrients are deficient and which are sufficient.
- **Water correctly.** Plant development can be harmed by either too much or too little water. Plants that are drought-stressed are more likely to attract spider mites.

EXAMINE **the plants for pests and correctly identify them.**

Learn to recognize the many insects and other critters that live in the garden. Many of them are advantageous. Plant pest issues can be identified with the aid of extension workers. Undiagnosed problems should not be treated.

PESTS MAY HARM garden plants at any stage of development, from seed to maturity. Inspect the plants for pests on a weekly or more frequent basis, keep track of natural enemies, and evaluate the effectiveness of pest management measures. Look for aphids, whiteflies, spider mites, and armyworm, Colorado potato beetle, and squash bug egg clusters on the undersides of leaves.

BEAT the plants on a piece of off-white paper to identify low populations of spider mites and thrips; the pests will fall off the plant and onto the paper, where they may be detected. Although yellow sticky cards are often advertised as insect repellents, they are best utilized to keep track of pest activities. The winged adult stages of aphids, leafminers, thrips, whiteflies, and many other flies are attracted to these cards. Pests should be discovered early and their numbers monitored; thus, cards should be inspected and changed. Many insect pests, particularly moths, can be monitored using pheromones, which are sex-attractive compounds.

TAKE into account all insect control options.
Consider preventative strategies and the best approach for lowering pest populations if a pest epidemic develops. **The following are some mechanical suppression techniques:**

- Reflective mulches, like foil paper, can help to keep pests like aphids at bay.
- Cutworm, sowbug, and pillbug barriers to protect young plants or transplants. Place a barrier around the base of each plant made of cardboard, plastic, or metal cans with the tops and bottoms removed.
- **Overlooking the garden are screens.** Even tiny insects like thrips will be unable to get through fine-mesh screens or textiles. There are a variety of goods to choose from. Insects can be kept out when

barriers are properly maintained; nevertheless, plants must still be inspected on a regular basis, which necessitates removing the barrier. Because the temperature inside barriers frequently surpasses the temperature outside, remove them before the plants become overheated. When the temperatures behind the screen are reasonable, this approach works best in the early spring or fall.
- **Trellises and cages.** Soil pests can affect plants growing on the ground. Cucumbers and tomatoes, for example, are easier to handle when grown on trellises or in cages. It's simpler to keep an eye on pests and spray plants when they're raised off the ground.
- **High-pressure water sprays.** With high-pressure water sprays focused on the undersides of leaves, you may remove small pests like aphids and spider mites from plants. There are commercial spray devices on the market, but comparable devices may also be manufactured at home. Be cautious not to damage the plant or spread bugs around the garden. Treatments may need to be repeated.

PROTECT bees by conserving natural enemies.

Natural enemies are the first line of defense against insect infestations. Other insects are preyed upon by spiders, praying mantids, lady beetles, ground beetles, green lacewings, ambush bugs, assassin bugs, minute pirate bugs, and several wasp species. Small parasitic wasps and flies, as well as bacteria, fungi, and viruses, are the most potent natural enemies.

. . .

ALLOW natural enemies to reduce the insect invasion instead of using pesticides as a last option. Select the least harmful, most target-specific types that disintegrate fast if a pesticide is necessary.

THESE CREATURES SHOULD BE FOSTERED, whether they are naturally existing or intentionally put into the garden. In order to control pests in the garden, natural enemies can be released. Lady beetles and green lacewing larvae eat aphids and whiteflies, predaceous mites eat two-spotted spider mites, and some wasps parasitize certain insect pests. (Trichogramma species are found in caterpillar eggs, whereas Encarsia species are found in young whiteflies.)

THE NUMBER OF PESTS PRESENT, the habitat, release timings, past pesticide usage, and the presence of ants can all impact the effects of these natural enemies. Parasitic nematodes can be used to manage a number of soil pests in vegetable gardens.

BEES ARE important for pollination cucumbers, pumpkins, squash, melons, and other protected crops. Pesticides should not be used during the hours when bees are active. Instead, spray plants early in the morning or late in the afternoon, when bees are less busy. Avoid using bee-toxic items or formulations. If a beehive is close, cover it during pesticide application or protect it from chemical drift.

ONLY USE **insecticides when absolutely necessary.**
If other methods of insect management have failed, a pesticide may be necessary. Pesticides are controlled by law and

must be applied rigorously according to label recommendations since they are hazardous and must be handled with caution.

RAISED BED GARDENING Triumphs Over Poor Soil Conditions

Think that the poor soil where you live means you're doomed to a life of gardening disasters? Think again. You can beat your soil problems by taking raising your plants out of the ground. Raised area gardening means you never have to worry about poor soil conditions and that you can have a healthy, thriving garden no matter where you live and what your soil type. Even if you have the world's best soil for growing, doing your gardening in raised beds still has some advantages. Find out more about the pros and cons of raised bed gardening and see if it is right for you.

FIRST THINGS FIRST - As the name suggests, raised bed gardening involves planting your plants in a bed off the ground rather than planting directly into the soil. Raised beds come in all different sizes, and there are many different kinds of receptacles for raised beds, depending on the size and where you want to hang the beds.

THE ABILITY TO manage the soil is one of the most significant benefits of using the raised bed. Because you choose and mix the ground yourself, you can create the perfect soil environment for the plants you want to grow. That means even if you're going to grow plants that don't typically thrive in your area because of your local soil composition, you can grow them in raised planters in which you have created the perfect soil for those plants.

. . .

THERE ARE other benefits to raised areas, even if the soil is not an issue in your area. Another significant advantage to consider is how the raised beds let you target the use of things you put on your garden. Apply fertilizer and mulch where they are needed - and there only - so you end up using less and do not accidentally apply these things where they are not required. If you use chemical pesticides, herbicides, or insecticides, you can use a smaller amount of them, and again, you can target their use. Because you apply them only to the raised bed, you don't have to worry about runoff or the effects these chemicals can have on your pets or kids who play in your yard. All in raised bed gardening makes for more efficient planting.

ONE GREAT BENEFIT of a raised gardening bed is the fact that the planting area is elevated. Since the garden is not ground level, it is much easier to tend. Garden enthusiasts with back problems will love being able to see their plants and manage them without bending over and dealing with hours of painful work. Raised areas are ideal for people with joint pain and injuries that make it difficult for them to garden traditionally.

ALTHOUGH RAISED garden beds have all of these benefits and make different kinds of gardening possible in areas where the soil is not ideal, the beds can't trump every problem a garden may face. For example, you still need to consider the climate in your area and choose plants accordingly - raised planters or not, and tropical plants won't grow in snowy climates. Also, you will still need to pay attention to what level of sunlight your garden area gets and choose your plants with that in mind.

. . .

FURTHER, although most people with raised beds deal with less pest infestation, you will still need some way to deal with plant-munching insects. Even though raised beds can't fix everything, however, they are still a great option when soil limits the way you garden.

GETTING THE SOIL Mix Right in Raised Bed Gardening

Are you adding some raised beds to your garden this year? Great idea. Many say that raised beds produce about four times the amount of produce as do row crops. Also, plants seem more vigorous in the early season, probably because the soil in a raised bed warms faster than in the garden patch. Gardeners love early season growth.

NONE OF THIS IS TRUE, of course, if the soil in your raised bed isn't at its best. And that's the great thing about raised beds. You can dig them out and fill them as you like. Think of them as a controlled experiment in which you're looking for just the perfect mix of organic materials — including beneficial microbes and other living things — and naturally occurring nutrients like nitrogen and minerals.

THE EASY WAY is to buy topsoil and compost, in bags or not, and fill up the bed's box. If you have your compost or can get reliable, organic compost — we were lucky to get it from a local, organic dairy goat farm — it's worth making your soil recipe. That way, you'll be able to fine-tune it for particular crops. Growing tomatoes? Make your soil slightly acidic, just the way they like it. Growing greens? You'll want to keep the nitrogen low until you have germination.

· · ·

If you're using compost, make sure that it's finished. If you're adding manures of any kind, make sure they're completely composted and are no longer "hot." Mix in other materials, like peat, pumice, or vermiculite if you're looking for good drainage, or sand, which root vegetables like. The easiest way to make sure compost is garden-ready is to spread it in the fall, leaving it on the surface to finish through the freeze and thaw cycles of winter.

If you didn't spread compost in the fall or just don't have any to spare, you can make it on the spot and grow in it as you do. We've stuck a bale or two of straw in raised beds in the fall, and we're left with good results when we pulled the remnants off in the spring.

Not only does the bale smother any weeds that might try to poke up early, but it also conditions the soil beneath where it sits. We even know someone that placed a bale right on the sod where they put their box in August and finished up with topsoil when it came time to plant next spring.

If you're putting in new raised beds this spring, why not put your first planting right in the straw bales? The craft of straw bale gardening has grown in popularity, and for a good reason. Some gardeners skip the box altogether and grow in the bale.

The Perfect Raised Bed Soil Mix (Weed-Free)

Good organic garden soil is the single most important ingredient for healthy, nutritious vegetables. It is loose and fluffy — filled with air that plant roots need — and has plenty of nutrients and minerals essential for vigorous plant growth and bountiful yields. Filling your raised beds is an opportunity to get high-quality soil and to fine-tune the mix of fertilizers and amendments.

The following soil mix was developed to fill a 4' X 8' raised bed one foot deep (32 cu ft).

    5 bags Black Gold Peat Moss, 2.2 cf x 5 = 11 cf
    3 bags Teufel's Organic Compost, 3 cf x 3 = 9 cf
    4 bags Worm Castings, 1 cf x 4 = 4 cf
    3 bags Organic Chicken Manure, 1 cf x 3 = 3 cf
    2 bag Therm-O-Rock Organic Vermiculite, 2 cf x 2 = 4 cf
    3-6 lbs Azomite
    1-2 lbs Kelp Meal
    3-6 lbs Oyster Shell Flour
    2-4 lbs All-Purpose Fertilizer

Have on hand all the ingredients for your soil mix before you start filling the beds, and pre-mix as much as possible on a large tarp if necessary to avoid pockets of peat, manure, or any other ingredients.

Note: Do NOT use pressure-treated wood or railroad ties for your raised bed frame because of chemical leaching.

Once the hay bale growing is over, your raised box will be left with good-quality left behind from the composted straw. You can hasten the process by adding some compost or topsoil, which you'll probably do as part of sticking plants in the bale. Either way, the soil inside your raised bed will benefit.

. . .

Bales provide good moisture control. They also warm faster in cool weather and insulate, if damp, in warm. And while you're growing cucumbers with the help of a little soil or compost out of the top, the bale is making soil for you on the bottom.

Not all bales are created equal. Baled hay and pasture cuttings will contain weed seeds, something that can bring problems into your garden. Straw, if it's what's left after seed heads have been harvested, usually contains little weed seed. The terms seem interchangeable at times. A glance at the bales you're buying should tell you which they are, no matter what they're being sold as.

Give Your Plants a Balanced Diet

Just like people, plants need a range of nutrients to thrive. If you make your compost, the leftovers from your balanced diet become food for your garden — but your kitchen compost is limited to the range of what your household commonly eats. Many gardening advisers recommend using at least five different sources of compost: for instance, your kitchen compost plus four different bags from a garden store. In addition, supplementing any known imbalances with targeted amendments leads to great rewards at harvest time.

An all-purpose organic fertilizer is the simplest way to go for the beginning gardener but armed with your soil test results; you may want to fine-tune your beds. **Essential nutrients for all plants include:**

- **Nitrogen:** provided abundantly by leguminous cover crops or composted manure.
- **Phosphorus:** rock phosphate and bone meal are both good sources.
- **Potassium:** kelp meal or greensand are long-lasting potassium releasers.
- **Calcium:** commonly supplied by gypsum or lime. Glacial rock dust provides calcium and other minerals while raising the pH of acidic soil.
- **Magnesium:** Epsom salts will raise magnesium without affecting pH, while dolomitic lime will raise both pH and magnesium.
- **Sulfur:** generally required only in alkaline soil. Adding sulfur will slowly lower pH through microbial action.

Gardening for years with a nutrient deficiency can be so discouraging that it's hard to stay enthusiastic. Though in the excitement of spring, it may be tempting to rush into planting with whatever dirt you have on hand, take your time. All your labor will be in vain without the appropriate soil foundation. Take steps now to ensure some positive reinforcement for your efforts!

9

EXTENDING YOUR SEASON OF RAISED BED VEGETABLE GARDEN

Few gardeners are satisfied with their growing season's duration. Tomatoes and melons hardly have enough time to mature in the far north. Drought and extreme heat in the South confine planting to the spring and fall seasons.

THE GOOD NEWS is that you can protect your plants from harsh weather and prolong your gardening season by two, three, or even six months by utilizing a few easy season-extending strategies and plant-protection equipment.

REDUCE **your exposure to the wind.**
If your garden plants must contend with high winds, they will use most of their energy to survive rather than build strong root systems and put on healthy growth. You may create a wood fence, plant a windbreak of trees and shrubs, or use windbreak netting to shelter your garden from the wind. It's not your objective to produce a dead calm; it's to lower the wind speed.

. . .

A FENCE on that side of the garden may be all that's needed if there's a prevailing wind direction. Try a temporary plastic mesh fence or cover your plants with polypropylene garden cloth, unique covers, or cold frames if setting up a permanent fence or hedge involves more time or money than you are willing to invest. Seedlings planted under the protection of garden cloth often grow twice as fast as control plants.

WARM UP THE SOIL.

If you mulched your garden during the winter, make careful to remove the mulch from the planting beds in the early spring to allow the soil to breathe. Raised beds are another technique to warm the soil fast. Covering chilly spring soil with black plastic can also raise the temperature of the soil by a few degrees. The plastic can be left on for the whole growing season or removed before planting.

MELONS and other heat-loving plants will benefit from a combination of black plastic mulch on the soil and plant coverings or garden cloth. In the fall, covering plants with a garden cloth will help retain heat and keep the soil several degrees warmer. Heat-loving crops like peppers, okra, and tomatoes may get a couple of weeks longer to mature as a result.

PROTECT yourself from the sun and the heat.

Hot weather is equally as difficult to deal with as cold weather. Excessive heat can stress and stunt young plants; salad greens become bitter and go to seed, and germinating seeds might be problematic. Shade netting keeps plants and soil cool while also aiding moisture retention. It may be directly applied to wire hoops or a moveable hardwood frame. The same thing may be done with a piece of wood lathe attached to a building.

SPRING AND FALL **frosts should be avoided.**

Frost is a limiting factor for most gardeners in the spring and fall. All but the hardiest garden crops will be killed by a single night of 32 degrees F. Garden cloth (or row coverings) is considerably simpler to handle and more effective than sheets, blankets, or cardboard boxes as emergency alternatives. These textiles come in a variety of thicknesses, and some can withstand temperatures as low as 25 degrees Fahrenheit.

COLD FRAMES and portable greenhouse structures can provide even better cold protection, allowing you to continue harvesting cold-weather crops well into the winter.

THREE METHODS **for Extending the Harvest**

CONSIDER the climate in your area first. How long do you want to make the season last, and how much time are you willing to put in? If you live in a cold climate and want to extend your harvest season all year, you'll need to invest in a greenhouse and be willing to give it daily attention. If you want a few additional weeks of ripe tomatoes in the fall and salads a couple of weeks sooner in the spring, the solution is simple and affordable.

- **The 30-day rule:** If you can create a sheltered growth environment where your seedlings are protected from the scorching sun, cold wind, frost, and insects, they will germinate much faster. For the first couple of weeks after transplanting, keep seedlings covered with garden cloth. Sun, air, and water permeable garden textiles made of spun polyester or polypropylene allow excess heat to leave and rainfall to pass through. All that's necessary is a weekly check for water and weeds on your plants.

ON WARM DAYS, the zippered top of this one-of-a-kind cover may be unzipped. Individual plants can be protected with clear plastic milk jugs, coffee cans with the ends cut off, or tomato cages. Simply make sure the cover is ventilated and keep an eye out for symptoms of overheating.

- **The 60-day stretch:** Using garden textiles in the spring and autumn can extend your harvest season by two months. Use them as indicated above in the spring, but use a thicker cloth to maintain soil heat and avoid frost damage to the leaves in the fall.

BECAUSE CERTAIN KINDS are better adapted to early- or late-season output, choosing the correct plant variety may make a big difference. Some broccoli cultivars, for example, flourish in cold spring soils but go to seed fast once the weather warms up. Others can withstand heat, while others flourish in the dim light and cold temperatures of late autumn.

- **A three-to-four-month period of time:** Protection

tents and greenhouses may extend your harvest virtually year-round in many regions of the nation. It's easier than you would think to maintain a protected growth environment in the face of wildly varying weather extremes. Salad greens in February and tomatoes all the way through Thanksgiving vastly exceed the initial outlay.

CONCENTRATING your energy is the key to success. Concentrate on a few crops or a specific area of your garden. The simplest to grow are salad greens and root crops. A 3 ft. by 4 ft. bed of greens may produce enough salads for several months. It's critical to select appropriate cultivars and stick to a consistent planting schedule.

GROWING UNDERCOVER GIVES them a whole new world of possibilities and great rewards. Imagine having a salad bar with fresh, organic food available eight or ten months of the year right outside your door.

Square Foot Gardening – Planting With Raised Bed Gardens

Learning how to garden by square foot is ideal for people who have a small backyard or are limited to gardening on their patio. It will help you to save space and teach you how to maximize what you have available. Square foot gardening is going to help you create works of art with limited space!

. . .

To start, you are going to create a raised bed typically. The most common size is 4x4 feet; however, you can custom fit this to any size you deem suitable, even as small as 1x1 ft. The width should be 4 to 6 inches. Raised beds are ideal because they will prevent people and pets from trampling the soil and plants. You do not want the soil trampled because it will cause it to become compacted. Compacted soil is more difficult to work with because it reduces oxygen flow.

Once you have your raised bed built and filled with the soil, you will want to divide it into sections. Typically these sections, or plots, will be one square foot. Section each plot off. This is going to help you to organize your garden and determine where to place your plants. When you follow a system like this, you will find you can plant a lot more than you thought possible.

One bonus of using a raised bed is that weeds are not as common. This is beneficial to you as you won't have to spend your time weeding your garden. Minimal maintenance is always welcomed!

Raised bed gardens do fine with compost or peat soil. These will hold water well and slowly release water, and they are great at holding nutrients that the plants will love. This means you won't have to water or fertilize as often. When you start a square foot garden, you will discover that it is easy to grow your organic veggies for you and your family to enjoy.

How Square Foot Gardening Can Save You Money

When you go to the nursery, it's all well and fine to buy your seedlings and plant them in your garden. But wouldn't it be easier and cheaper if you could learn how to do this yourself without going to the nursery in the first place?

SEED GARDENING IS EASY, rewarding, and will certainly save you money. This is where square foot gardening techniques really come to the fore, as you can garden in a limited space to grow and raise your seedlings in a small box before planting them out.

HERE'S HOW TO DO IT:
First, you will need to buy or make a container approximately 1-foot square. You can use timber if you wish, or you can use an old fruit box you have lying around, or even a polystyrene box will do. Next, you need to purchase some seed-raising mixture. This is especially nurturing sandy-based soil, which will allow you to grow from seeds easily. The second step is to have the seas themselves! You can get these from a nursery in packets or harvest them yourself from other vegetables that have gone to seed in your garden.

GENTLY TAMP down the soil to make sure it is not too loose. The tiny seedlings need a fairly tight space for the roots to latch onto; that is why making the soil reasonably compact is a vital first step. Just think like a seed! Now you can scatter the seeds over the surface of this prepared bed, then lightly sprinkle a layer of potting soil over the top of the seeds, then water everything in.

. . .

THE SEED TRAYS CAN NOW be placed wherever you like, usually in a protected area with a little bit of sun and even light. The important thing is to keep them well watered, at least to keep the soil moist, as this encourages the seeds to grow even better.

DEPENDING UPON THE seeds you have sewn, you may find that they are quite tightly spaced once they have begun to sprout. Do not be concerned at this point because you can thin them out after they are fully grown as you plant them. This will not always occur, but with larger plants like lettuces, it is more common than carrots.

ONCE YOUR FIRST seed tray is alive with new plants, you can think back and price each one you see with the nursery price, and that is how much you have saved. You will find that one seed tray, which has cost you may be four or five dollars, will have around 30 or 40 seedlings which you would have paid three or four dollars each. That means one tray can save you close to $100.

10
WAIST-HIGH RAISED BED GARDENING – GARDENING WITH ARTHRITIS

If you are one of the more than 27 million people afflicted with the pain from arthritis, you know firsthand how debilitating it is. Kneeling to plant impatiens has become torture, and the simple act of bending over to deadhead a marigold is frequently impossible.

So what do you do when you love gardening, but arthritis has put you on the sidelines?

Stop bending or kneeling in the garden. And container gardening in raised beds or planters is one way to achieve a no-bend garden.

Maybe you injured your back and neck. Bending and kneeling to plant, weed or water became excruciating, and you start thinking about what you could do to keep gardening but maintain a more pain-free existence.

. . .

WAIST-HIGH RAISED bed gardening is the answer. This will eliminate the bending, and kneeling movement from your garden routine made the act of being in your garden a joy again.

THE WAY to do this is to make sure that you plant in tall enough containers or place your container gardens on a roughly waist-high surface. If you're used to planting in large containers, ask a member of your family to either place the planter on a platform or, better yet, on wheels so you can easily move the planting around.

FIND A PLACE TO put your containers to start working on your new waist-high garden. Do you have a wall or a table that's nearby? Use those surfaces to help get your plants up to a level that's comfortable for you.

AN ALTERNATIVE TO waist-high raised bed gardening is to get a stool or chair you can use for planting. It's never going to be the same as when you could bend and kneel with ease, but some gardening has always been better than none for me.

USING HANGING plants is also another possibility. Potting them in a hanging planter and using a hose to water should keep you from bending and kneeling. You can garden even with arthritis if you take a moment to think about the possibilities.

Garden With Ease With a Waist High Gardening Box

Gardening is an enjoyable, healthy hobby for all, especially those who love the feel of the sunshine on their faces, the rich black soil in their hands, and the wafting scent of growing plants and flowers. Their fragrance is heady, intoxicating, and irresistible. If you grow to produce, the fruits of your labors bring many rewards along with the knowledge you are giving your family the freshest, safest, and nutritionally dense produce available. Sadly though, gardening can become almost unbearable for those with limited mobility or those who endure chronic pain and stiffness due to fibromyalgia, arthritis, or other situations which make bending, standing, and weeding difficult, if not impossible. If you are suffering from any of these, the waist-high garden box is a much-needed invention.

Easy to build, long-lasting, easily accessible, and portable, the waist-high gardening box brings back the joy of gardening. Consisting of two plastic tubs measuring three feet long by two feet wide, there is ample room for plants to grow and thrive. Some gardeners add on trellises for vining plants such as peas or situate their boxes against a deck railing, plant cucumbers, or other trailing plants.

Because of the ease of portability, waist-high garden boxes may be moved to any area you desire. If you need constant sunshine on your veggies or a little more shade on your impatiens, there is always an ideal location and a simple move to rectify the situation. Accessing your garden box is easier when it is adjustable for height comfort. Whether you are in a wheelchair, a first-time gardener, or a child, the height adjustments can be made so that it is a perfect fit for you.

CHILDREN ESPECIALLY LOVE TO GARDEN. They have a keen interest in watching as each plant they chose grows larger each day until finally, it is time to harvest the results of their efforts. Mealtime is more fun when a child has been allowed to grow his/her produce, as he/she will more readily want to taste it.

WHETHER YOU ARE a first-time or experienced gardener, have limited mobility, are in a wheelchair, or have children, a waist-high garden box will give you ease of use for the seasons to come.

COMPANION PLANTING

Have you heard the term "carrots love tomatoes"? That old adage relates to the concept that growing these two popular veggies together will frequently boost both of their yields, making your plants happier, healthier, and more robust.

GARDENERS HAVE KNOWN for as long as there have been crops that work together to improve yields. Scientists have lately investigated the phenomena to learn more about what happens when plants coexist. Companion planting, they've learned, **can help in the following ways:**

- More fragile plants might benefit from the presence of hardier species, which can protect them from the heat, wind, and heavy rains if placed close.
- **Improving pollination:** Plants with spectacular

flowers, strong scents, or other attractants can attract pollinating insects to plants that need pollination nearby. Plants that attract helpful insects aid agricultural growth.
- **Pest trapping and luring:** Planting pest-attracting types in the garden will help pests stay away from delicious, valued veggies and other plants. This is referred to as "trap cropping."
- **Pest repellent:** Many plants generate chemicals in their leaves and roots that naturally repel pests.
- **Enriching the soil:** As plants break down or fix nitrogen from the atmosphere, they return important nutrients to the soil.

Companion Planting Benefits

Planting various crops together **has a number of advantages:**

- **Insect repellents and critter deterrents:** Some plants are insect repellents or animal deterrents. Garlic, for example, has an unpleasant odor that repels many pests.
- **Beneficial insects attracted:** Some plants also attract beneficial insects. Borage, for example, attracts pollinating bees and small pest-eating wasps.
- Large plants offer shade for smaller plants that need shelter from the sun, such as lettuce, which is shaded by maize.
- Tall plants, such as maize and sunflowers, can provide natural supports for lower-growing, spreading crops like cucumbers and peas.

- **Plant health:** When one plant absorbs specific chemicals from the soil, the soil biochemistry may alter in favor of adjacent plants.
- **Improving soil fertility:** Some crops, such as beans, peas, and other legumes, aid in the availability of nitrogen in the soil. Plants with lengthy taproots, such as burdock transport nutrients from deep within the soil to the surface, replenishing the topsoil for shallow-rooted plants.
- **Weed control:** Planting spreading crops like potatoes with tall, upright plants reduces the amount of open space where weeds thrive.

Popular Vegetable Companion Plants

Some of the greatest companion planting options for your garden are as follows:

- Basil attracts bees, which enhances pollination, tomato health, and flavor while repelling whiteflies, mosquitoes, spider mites, and aphids. Basil also repels whiteflies, mosquitoes, spider mites, and aphids.
- Insects are drawn away from tomatoes by parsley. Plant these herbs in the same row as the tomatoes.
- Borage attracts pollinating bees and small pest-eating wasps, and it goes great with tomatoes. Borage complements strawberries nicely, adding to their taste and vitality.
- Sage is a useful plant for warding off carrot fly. It's also a good idea to put it around a cabbage patch to keep cabbage moths away.
- Aphids, ants, and flea beetles are all deterred by the

- mint. Plant mint close in its pot or bed, but keep in mind that it is a very aggressive growth!
- Aphids, onion flies, ermine moths, and Japanese beetles are all deterred by garlic and garlic spray. Cabbage, cane fruits, fruit trees (particularly peaches), roses, and tomatoes are among the plants that benefit from it. Late potato blight can be avoided by drinking garlic tea.
- Hoverflies are attracted to poached eggplants (a wildflower), which reduce aphids on neighboring lettuce.
- Crimson clover planted with broccoli was shown to increase the number of local spiders, which helped to manage pests.
- Tansy protects asparagus, bean, cabbage, carrot, celery, maize, lettuce, pea, pepper, potato, and tomato plants against cutworm. Nasturtiums drive hungry caterpillars away from brassicas like cabbage and broccoli and blackflies away from fava beans. (Plant tansy in pots like mint because it is considered invasive in some places.)
- Sunflowers go well with cucumbers and pole beans because they give support for climbing plants and shade for crops that can get sun-stressed in hotter areas.

Avoid **these combinations**

Certain plants sown close together might have a detrimental effect on each other. Gardeners have discovered **the following frequent garden enemies:**

- Beans and peas with garlic (and other alliums)

- Carrots and other members of this family with dill
- Cucumbers and herbs with a pleasant scent
- Potatoes with spinach
- Pole beans with beets

The Best Recommendations for Raised Bed Gardening

Here are a few ideas for **raised garden bed pairings:**

- *Tomatoes, onions, and garlic, with basil*

Many common pests, such as slugs and snails, are repelled by onions and garlic planted with tomatoes. Basil planted in the same bed as mature tomatoes might assist in enhancing their flavor.

- *Cabbage, radishes, and marigolds are a delicious combination.*

Cabbage maggots are often attacked by radishes and marigolds, so planting them with cabbages helps reduce them. If you have a slug problem, add some chives to this bed.

- *Carrots, lettuce, and chives*

Carrot rust flies are reported to be repelled by lettuce grown in and around them. Aphids and flea beetles are deterred from sucking the life out of your lettuce by chives. They also work to keep the carrot rust fly at bay.

- *Squash, runner beans, and corn are a delicious combination.*

THIS CLASSIC COMBINATION, known as the Three Sisters, is a win-win-win. Interplanting squash with maize and beans, which prevent common squash pests, is beneficial. Raccoons flee the thorny squash vines, leaving your corn alone—runner beans blossom, drawing pollinating insects to your squash, which require pollination to grow fruit. Finally, the corn provides a natural trellis for the vine-like beans.

- *Beets, kale, and bush beans*

ANOTHER METHOD TO pair plants is to think about where they are in the soil profile. While beets have deep roots that nourish your garden, bush beans and kale have shorter roots and won't compete for nutrients as much as another root crop. They also return important nutrients to the soil and are harvested faster than beets. However, pole beans and beets are known to be incompatible, so don't grow them together.

MAKE notes throughout the season on how it's working in your unique space under your garden's specific set of conditions if something isn't working as well as it should adjust as necessary with the knowledge that you're participating in an age-old practice, whatever pairings you choose for your raised garden beds.

Different Methods for Watering Raised Bed Gardens

Did you know that you may water crops on raised beds in a variety of ways to influence their growth? Each watering strategy has its own set of advantages and disadvantages, which might vary based on your crops.

- *Manual Watering*

THIS IS the simplest and most cost-effective way to irrigate your raised bed garden vegetables. You may use a tiny bowl to pour water over your plants and break the force of the water with your palm. You may also use a sprinkle nozzle on a watering can.

MANUAL WATERING ALLOWS you to measure how much water you feed your plants easily, but it is time and energy-demanding. Because hand watering takes human effort, you may need to adjust your schedule, get up early, or make other arrangements to water your plants when they need it most.

- *Garden Hoses*

INSTEAD OF A WATERING CONTAINER, you may always use a garden hose. If your plants are young and delicate, avoid immediately watering them with the hose.

TO AVOID DAMAGING your plants with solid water pressure, use a hose with a perforated nozzle and choose a gentler, lower pressure setting.

. . .

You may simply lay the hose on the ground and let it drain into the raised bed.

- *Sprinklers*

Sprinklers are a simple and enjoyable way to water raised bed gardening. Sprinklers deliver a consistent amount of water to the crops in their immediate vicinity.

Remember to place your sprinklers in such a way that each plant receives an equal amount of water.

For your raised bed crops, water from sprinklers should reach both the leaves and the roots or base of the plants. To guarantee even watering in your raised bed garden, you may use multiple sprinklers.

- *Drip Lines*

Drip lines are excellent for raised beds since they provide more than simply water. They can also be used to divide the raised bed or to give the planting area greater form and definition.

Drip lines deliver a steady stream of water at low pressure via perforations in the hose line.

. . .

PLACE the drip line near your plants so that water can reach their lower roots, which can be up to 12 inches deep. Drip lines should be used for 15 to 30 minutes every watering session.

WHEN UTILIZING DRIP LINES, be careful not to overwater your plants. It's difficult to tell if the plants are getting too much water because they supply tiny quantities of water all the time.

- *Furrows*

FURROWS ARE large ditches excavated in the earth for planting or watering crops in the vicinity.

IF YOU WANT to make gardening more convenient for yourself, build a furrow in your raised bed that links all of the plants.

WATER WILL FLOW through the dug-out channels to other sections of the garden if you pour water on an elevated part of the furrow. This allows water to be delivered to all of the plants in the raised bed from a single source.

When Should Raised Beds Be Watered?

Depending on your plants, the best time to water raised beds is either early in the morning or late in the evening.

PLANTS SHOULD NOT BE WATERED in direct sunlight. When watering with automatic systems like sprinklers or drip lines, keep this in mind, and consider using a timer to control it.

- *Early Morning Watering*

WATERING plants early in the morning is also suggested since the ambient temperature and the water temperature is comparable at that time of day.

YOUR PLANTS WILL NOT BE STARTLED when you water them this way.

- *Late Evening Watering*

PLANTS REQUIRE MORE water during the hotter parts of the day when the sun dries them out. Plants gather water from the ground during the day, and with the aid of the sun, the water departs via the leaves (a process known as transpiration).

PLANTS NEED energy from the sun and water to obtain nutrients at night. Plants employ osmosis to acquire nutrients from the earth when the temperature is cold and steady at night.

PLANTS CANNOT GATHER as many nutrients as they should if there isn't enough water in the soil. Make sure the earth isn't parched at night.

- *Avoid watering in the middle of the day.*

You should not water your plants during the daytime, especially on a sunny afternoon, unless you water them more than three times daily or use sprinklers, drip lines, or other automatic techniques.

If you only water your plants once a day, you should avoid watering them when they are in direct sunlight. Before it has a chance to sink into the soil, the water will quickly evaporate.

Your plants will be stunned by the temperature differential between cool or cold water and ambient temperature if the air temperature or heat from the sun is extreme.

If you need to water your plants in the afternoon or in direct sunlight, use sprinklers, drip lines, or water them periodically to keep the soil moist.

How Often Should a Raised Bed Garden Be Watered?

When it comes to maintaining a raised bed garden, watering frequently is critical. **Consider the following variables when deciding how often to water your plants:**

- **Location:** If you live in a dry climate, you'll need to water your raised bed as frequently as possible to keep the soil moist. You will need to water your raised bed less frequently if you reside in a wet area.
- **Season:** Water your raised beds on a regular basis during dry seasons, such as the summer. To avoid overwatering in the fall, consider the rain while watering your raised bed.

- **Plants:** How often you water the plants in your raised bed is determined by the type of plants you have. Tomatoes and cucumbers, for example, require more water than root vegetables like potatoes and radishes.
- **Water Drainage Quality:** You may need to water your raised bed more frequently if it drains water fast. Never let the soil become completely dry.

How to Improve Raised Bed Garden Water Retention and Drainage

Understanding and optimizing your raised bed's water drainage can also impact how frequently you need to water your plants. Keep the following points in mind when seeking to enhance your raised bed garden's water retention or drainage.

WATER RETENTION ENHANCEMENT

Raised bed gardens should, in theory, drain water rapidly. **Consider utilizing the following garden items to help retain water:**

- **Mulch:** Mulch reduces water loss due to evaporation by blocking sunlight from reaching the soil. Mulching also helps to keep weeds out of the raised bed garden.
- **Liners:** Liners such as newspapers, cardboards, weed textiles, and plastics can prevent water from draining since water cannot travel through them readily (or at all). If you utilize a liner, you should water your raised bed garden less frequently to avoid overwatering.

WATER DRAINAGE IMPROVEMENTS

If your raised bed garden is retaining too much water, you might want to try some of these drainage techniques.

- **Add rock layers to the soil:** Adding rock layers to the soil can help the water drain more quickly. You may add pebbles on the ground before pouring dirt over them for your plants while constructing your raised bed.
- **Increase the number of plants:** The more crops you put in your raised bed, the more water you'll need to use. Growing additional crops will help to minimize the quantity of water that remains in your raised bed.

Signs of Improper Watering in a Raised Bed Garden

Overwatering

You'll notice symptoms in your yard if you're overwatering your raised bed, **such as:**

- Algae development
- Soggy soil
- Roots rot
- Stunted plant growth
- Dark brown tips on the plant's leaves.
- Plats with completely wilted, browning, or fallen leaves

Underwatering

If you see any of the following, your raised bed garden is not being watered as often as it **should be:**

- The soil rapidly dries out.
- Stunted plant growth
- Plants with yellowing green leaves
- Plants with withering leaves, stems, and roots that are dry

WHEN SHOULD Your Garden Be Fertilized?

Before planting edible crops, fertilizer is generally sprayed in the spring and blended with the garden soil. You may still carefully massage granular fertilizer (not liquid fertilizer, which can burn young roots) around the plants if you've already sowed your seeds or planted seedlings. It doesn't need to be worked deeply into the soil; the top 3 to 5 inches would suffice. Then add the fertilizer and water it in.

FERTILIZE perennial blooming plants before they begin to develop in the spring. Wait until the ground is no longer frozen and your final frost date is less than a week away. This reduces the likelihood of frost killing the weak new growth brought on by the fertilizer.

WHILE A SPRING APPLICATION is a solid rule of thumb, know which plants require assistance when they are growing the most.

- For lettuce, arugula, kale, and other leafy greens, this happens early in the spring.

- Corn and squash grow quickly in the middle of the summer. Many gardeners use a tiny quantity of fertilizer as a beginning at the time of sowing for a long-season crop like corn, and then a bigger dose in early summer, just before the period of fast foliar development.
- Tomatoes and potatoes will require more fertilizer in the middle of the season as the plants absorb and utilize current nutrients. Switch to a low-nitrogen fertilizer when tomatoes begin to blossom to encourage more flowers and fruit rather than foliage.
- The time for perennial plants is determined by the plant's growth cycle. Blueberries, for example, benefit from a fertilizer applied at bud break early in the season, but June-bearing strawberries benefit from a fertilizer applied after harvest.
- As dormancy breaks at the start of the growing season, ornamental trees, shrubs, and perennials are frequently fertilized.

Take a soil test every time!

A "soil test" is the only technique to assess the number of nutrients in your soil accurately. You'll have plenty of time to obtain the results if you test in the autumn. Your local cooperative extension generally offers soil tests for free or at a moderate cost. This isn't something you'll have to do every year. The aim is to understand your soil, build it up, and apply fertilizer to it every year to maintain the fundamental fertility level.

· · ·

You may even discover that your garden contains high amounts of nutrients if it has been fertilized for years. If your soil already has a lot of nutrients, you don't want to add more; this can stifle your plants' development.

What Kind of Fertilizer Should I Use, and How Much of It?

A fertilizer bag will have a numerical combination such as 3-4-4, 8-24-8, or 12-12-12 on it. Nitrogen (N), Phosphorus (P), and Potassium (K) are the three most important nutrients that plants require (K). The figures represent the proportion of each nutrient's weight in the bag. When you combine the figures together, you get the proportion of the bag's overall weight (the rest is simply filler to make it easy to apply). Other nutrients, such as calcium, magnesium, iron, and manganese may also be present.

Use a basic vegetable fertilizer to get your garden started. You can use a 3-4-4 number herb and vegetable plant food for veggies. In order to help avoid blossom-end rot, you can use a special fertilizer with a 3-4-6 ratio, including calcium for tomatoes.

Phosphorous is vital since it is required for root growth and development. Potassium improves the ability of plants to withstand illness. It's worth noting that the nitrogen (first number) is lower. Have you ever come across tomato plants with beautiful foliage but no blooms or fruit? This is due to an excess of nitrogen, which promotes leafy development.

. . .

After a period of significant development or fruiting, vegetable crops require the majority of their nitrogen. Too much nitrogen before this period slows maturity, lowers blooming, and diminishes yields. The decomposition of organic materials in your soil will also provide nitrogen to your plants.

Some plants benefit from nitrogen side treatments later in the season (sprinkled in the middle of rows). The plant's requirement for nitrogen frequently surpasses what the first two can provide, necessitating a nitrogen side-dressing. However, it is dependent on the vegetable.

- Three weeks after transplanting, cabbage, cauliflower, and broccoli might benefit from additional fertilizer.
- After blooming, peas, beans, cucumbers, and muskmelons can benefit.
- After the first fruit sets, peppers, eggplants, and tomatoes benefit, and tomatoes may use more approximately two weeks after selecting your first tomato and then again a month later.
- When sweet corn plants are 8 to 10 inches tall, and one week after tassels develop, they can benefit.
- When plants are roughly one-third grown, spinach, kale, mustard, and turnip greens can benefit.
- Sweet potatoes, watermelons, carrots, beets, turnips, parsnips, and lettuce should not have any nitrogen added to them.

The amount of fertilizer to use per 1,000 square feet of garden space should be specified on the fertilizer package. If you need assistance translating to your garden space, you can always ask the nursery staff.

. . .

ORGANIC VS. PROCESSED **Fertilizers**

Both processed and organic fertilizers are subject to fertilizer standards.

NATURAL COMPONENTS such as phosphate rock (P), sodium chloride (NaCl), and potassium chloride (KCl) salts are used to make processed fertilizers (also known as "synthetic" or "chemical" fertilizers). These are still tweaked to make them more concentrated. Most (but not all) processed fertilizers are quick-release in a water-soluble form, allowing nutrients to reach the plant rapidly, which can be beneficial in some cases.

ORGANIC FERTILIZERS ARE plant-based products that gently release nutrients when soil microorganisms break them down. Most organic fertilizers, which are often administered in granular form (spread over the soil), are slow-release, adding organic material to the soil so that you don't have to apply it as frequently. (Plus, unlike many synthetic, water-soluble fertilizers that plants can't completely take, they don't leak into and contaminate rivers.) While the majority of organic fertilizers are slow-release, some do release a portion of their nutrients fast (animal manure, biosolids, and fish emulsion).

THE NUTRIENTS in processed and organic fertilizers are chemically identical. Slow is the way to go in the ideal world.

IN TERMS OF COST, while organic fertilizers are more expensive upfront than processed fertilizers, they are frequently nonetheless cost-effective for small plots. You also don't have to apply as frequently. Organic surpasses processed when it comes to the long-term advantages to your soil.

How to Apply Granular Fertilizer

Apply granular fertilizers by distributing them over a large area, either by hand or with a spreader, for that first "starter" fertilizer treatment of the season. Alternatively, if you've already planted, apply fertilizer along the rows. In order to help the fertilizer seep down toward the plants' root zones, all dry fertilizers should be worked or moistened into the top 3 to 5 inches of soil with hoe or spadework after application. If your plants have already begun to develop, nurture them to avoid damaging the roots.

Lighter supplemental treatments can be provided to the top inch of soil in crop rows and perennial beds, as well as around the drip lines of trees and shrubs, during the growing season.

In general, applying granular fertilizers right before a good rain can help the fertilizer make its way down into the soil where roots can reach it.

How to Apply Liquid Fertilizers

All water-soluble fertilizers are applied by dissolving the substance in irrigation water and then sprinkling it on the plant's leaves and surrounding soil.

. . .

Don't use liquid fertilizer at the same time as you're planting! Some root hairs will break no matter how carefully you take plants from their pots and set them in the ground. The fertilizer will instantly reach the roots and penetrate them at the damaged places, perhaps "scorching" them and causing more die-back.

Many gardeners wait 2 to 3 weeks after planting before fertilizing with liquid solutions; by that time, any root damage to the freshly planted plants should have healed.

If the soil is dry, it is important to hydrate the plants thoroughly with plain water before applying the liquid fertilizer to avoid scorching the roots. Also, make sure the fertilizer is diluted according to the directions, or the leaves may burn. You may use an injector device to run fertilizer through a watering system if you have one.

When using liquid sprays, apply them on dry days early in the morning or late in the evening, when the leaves will have time to absorb the substance. On hot days when the vegetation is at risk of burning, stay indoors.

Garden Life After the Summer Harvest

You've gathered the final basket of tomatoes from your summer garden and plucked every pepper. So, what's next?

Your edible garden's ability to perform effectively in the future is largely determined by how well you care for it at the end of the season. This post-harvest garden care guide will help you set up your edible garden for success for years to come, including how to refill soil nutrients, when to mulch, which plants not to compost, and more.

- *Complete the harvest.*

Pick any remaining fruit, vegetables, and edible leaves when you're ready to complete your summer garden. Many fruits, such as tomatoes, continue to mature even after they've been picked. Make preparations to preserve, freeze, or give away extra food at the end of the summer.

In the winter, utilize dry herbs like thyme, basil, lavender, and rosemary. Allow the fruits to mature and dry on the vine before harvesting and saving the beans and squash seeds. Keep the seeds in a well-labeled jar or envelope in a dry, low-moisture environment.

- *Get rid of any summer edibles, diseased plants, or weeds.*

Remove any remaining fruits and seeds from the plants and discard them in the garden. If you have a compost pile, you may add the plants to it or put them in the green trash bin. (Starting composting in the fall is a fantastic idea.) Any plants that exhibit indications of illness should be removed and discarded. Powdery mildew, which appears as dusty white patches on leaves, should be disposed of in the garbage or yard waste bin, not the compost pile.

. . .

Remove weeds hidden behind summer plants with your hands or a garden hoe once the soil has been revealed.

Weeds that have not yet produced seeds can be composted; those that have already produced seeds should be discarded.

- *Clean and empty the pots.*

Remove weary or fading summer herbs and vegetable plants from containers after gathering any remaining fruit or edible leaves.

You can pour the dirt from the pots onto the compost pile or garden beds if the plants show no indications of illness. With a rake, spread out the soil and remove any root balls by hand.

Clean pots with a brush and a vinegar-and-soapy-water solution. Fill them with fresh potting soil for new cool-season plants and store them upside down in a protected place until next spring.

- *Replace nutrients in the soil.*

The key to having a healthy and profitable food garden year after year is good soil. Your herbs and vegetables have been soaking up soil minerals for months in order to power their development and fruit production this summer. The plants will not grow as tall or produce as many fruits and vegetables if you plant the same crops in the same soil the next year without adding nutrients back to the soil. You may keep a healthy edible garden season after season if you take care of the soil and restore its nutrients.

AMENDMENTS TO THE SOIL. If you have any homemade compost on hand, now is the time to utilize it. You may also get bagged compost from your neighborhood nursery. Organic fertilizers that restore nitrogen, phosphorus, and potassium for specific crops are also available. Cover the top layer of soil with a heavy layer of compost. Other changes can be made as needed, according to the package's instructions.

IF TAKING out plants made your soil feel heavy, adding extra organic material, such as compost, straw, or fully dried leaves, may help.

AFTER ADDING COMPOST, soil amendments, and any other organic material, turn over with a shovel, working everything into the soil.

IF YOU LIVE in a moderate winter climate, now is a good time to replant beds with cool-season crops like peas, carrots, and cabbages. Allow the beds to rest until spring planting in colder climates.

COVER CROPS ARE a type of crop that is used to hide Cover crops can also be used to restore nutrients to the soil. Cover crops enhance soil texture, reduce erosion, suppress weeds, and contribute important nutrients to the soil wherever they are planted, among other things.

THE PURPOSE of a cover crop is not to harvest it. Its main goal is to restore soil minerals and organic matter without using additional fertilizers. Cover crops include ryegrass, oats, barley, clover, and nitrogen-fixing legumes. Planting a cover crop will take a bed out of the rotation for a season, but it will make the soil healthier for the next planting season.

FAVA BEANS, as seen above, are a simple cover crop to experiment with within a small garden. Plant favas in a bed, let them develop pods for harvest (if you wish to eat them), and then trim or mow the plants in the bed, leaving the fallen cuttings to remain on the soil's surface. As a type of "green manure." Two to three weeks before spring planting, till organic materials into the soil to allow it to break down and enrich the soil.

- *Apply mulch.*

SPREAD A LAYER OF BARK, straw, or dried leaf mulch over the soil's surface if you're not utilizing a cover crop this winter. Mulch will assist prevent weed development, keep the soil warm for freshly planted cool-season crops, and keep the soil wet.

- *Pruning vines, brambles, and other perennial plants.*

ON GRAPES, kiwis, and other fruit vines, prune down thin or straggly vines, undesirable side shoots, and bigger vines.

CHOOSE four to six of the healthiest, most robust canes from each plant of brambles, such as blackberries, boysenberries, and raspberries, and cut the rest to the ground.

STRAWBERRY BEDS MAY BE THINNED by splitting plants and replanting them in rich, well-draining soil with plenty of areas to spread out. Cut down asparagus and artichokes to approximately 6 inches above the ground when they begin to die back naturally at the end of the season.

- *Perennials should be fertilized and mulched.*

GRAPES, brambles, strawberries, asparagus, and artichokes, for example, benefit from a coating of organic or synthetic fertilizer placed at the base of each plant, as well as a covering of bark or straw mulch to protect them from the harsh winter temperatures.

- *Cleaning and storing garden tools and supplies.*

OVER THE WINTER, keep trellises, tomato cages, and other garden materials stored in a garden shed or covered area. Organize your tools and tidy them up at the end of the season.

TO PREVENT the transmission of infections, dip the metal portions of shovels, spades, hand trowels, and pruning shears in a weak bleach solution and wipe dry. Sharpen any tool blades that need to be sharpened. To prevent rust and keep handles moist, apply a thin coat of oil to both the metal and wooden portions of the tools. In a garden shed, garage, or covered space, keep tools.

- *Make a New Year's resolution.*

DON'T FORGET to jot down ideas for next year's warm-weather edible garden. Consider your favorite plant types and your most successful plants. Were there any plants that didn't quite make it? Could adding more pollinator-friendly plants to your next food garden help? If that's the case, consider planting them around the perimeter. Make a list of these garden ideas now so you can plan for success next spring.

TAKING Care of Your Garden

Weeds are kept to a minimum by planting. You may need to weed a bit every week in the early spring, but by midsummer, your weeding duties should be done. When weeds do appear, pull them out as soon as possible, so your vegetable plants don't have to compete for moisture, nutrients, or root space.

IN A RAISED BED, the soil does not dry up as quickly as it does in a typical garden. The bed's edges assist in keeping moisture in the soil, while the plants shade the soil to decrease evaporation. Except in hot weather and droughts, your watering duties should be modest once your plants are well-established.

CROPS THAT TAKE three or four months to mature generally benefit from a second fertilizer treatment in the middle of the season. A monthly dose of water-soluble fertilizer, especially one containing humic acid, seaweed, and fish emulsion, is beneficial to almost all plants. These water-soluble nutrients are quickly absorbed by plants and aid in their health during stressful times. This is a simple approach to reduce insect and disease issues.

As soon as your garden appears to be ready to eat, you may begin harvesting it. At or near the height of maturity, crops are generally the tastiest and most nutritious. Remove any damaged or diseased plant material, as well as any wasted fruit or leaves. Keep an eye out for pests and take care of any problems right away.

To grow properly and provide a healthy yield, some plants, such as pole beans and most tomatoes, require a cage, trellis, or other kinds of support.

CONCLUSION

Gardening may be a rewarding experience. It can help you save hundreds of dollars on groceries each month while still providing your family with healthy, organic fruit.

Every gardener wants to see a return on their investment of time and money each year. Companion planting is a practice that can help you get the most out of your investment by improving yields, minimizing pests, and preserving soil quality. You can also use urban beekeeping to increase the health of your garden. The more bees that visit your garden, the more fruits and veggies you will produce.

Traditional in-ground gardens are wonderful, but there's something to be said for raised bed gardens, which allow you to grow more food in less space, customize the soil to your specific needs, and reduce the amount of space available for weeds to grow wild. In addition, the soil in a raised bed heats up faster in the spring than soil in an in-ground garden bed, allowing you to start planting sooner. They make it possible to plant without having to contend with stones and roots, and the soil in them is simple to amend each season.

When combined with low tunnels, raised beds to help extend the growing season when frost is a problem.

Raised bed gardens do, however, have a few disadvantages. They tend to dry out quickly in hot, dry weather. For whatever reason, roaming cats may find the pleasant, fluffy soil appealing. Additionally, when building a raised bed, keep in mind the width to guarantee that you can easily reach the middle when planting or maintaining your garden. However, with a little planning and protection, these few disadvantages can be easily avoided.

- **Don't walk on the soil.**

The light, fluffy, perfectly ideal soil you may generate with raised bed gardening is the most significant advantage. Build your raised beds in such a way that you can reach every section of them without having to stand in them. If you already have a raised bed and need to walk on parts of it, consider strategically placing patio pavers or boards and stepping on those instead of on the dirt.

- **Mulch after planting.**

After you've planted your garden, mulch it with straw, grass clippings, leaves, or wood chips. This will cut down on weeding time while also keeping the soil hydrated.

- **Make a plan for your irrigation system.**

Irrigating a raised bed with a soaker hose or drip irrigation is the best option. You may save yourself a lot of time and effort later on if you plan ahead of time and set up your irrigation system before planting.

- **Install a root and weed barrier.**

Place your raised bed away from the shade and roots of any huge trees in the region. To produce a productive crop, most vegetables like the full or partial sun. Consider putting a barrier at the bottom of the bed to prevent weeds from sprouting up through your new soil. A professional weed barrier or a thick piece of corrugated cardboard could be used.

If you already have a raised bed and are always fighting tree roots, you may wish to excavate the soil and move the raised bed to a better site. If you want to keep voles out of your garden, line the bottom and inside sides of your raised bed with hardware cloth before filling it with dirt. Due to the metal, mesh-like barrier, burrowing critters will find it nearly impossible to access the bed from below, where they consume the plant roots.

- **Compost top-dressing once a year**

In many ways, growing in a raised bed is similar to gardening in a huge container. The soil will settle and diminish over time, just like any other container garden. This can be avoided by applying a 1- to 2-inch layer of compost or composted manure before planting in the spring.

- **Fluff the soil as needed**

Stick a garden fork as deep as possible into the soil and twist it back and forth to soften compacted dirt in your raised bed between seasons. Do this all over the bed at 8- to 12-inch intervals, and the soil will be nicely loosened without a lot of back-breaking labor.

- **Even if you're not gardening, keep your soil covered.**

Apply a layer of organic mulch or sow a cover crop at the end of the growing season. Soil that has been exposed to harsh winter weather can break down and compact considerably more quickly than soil that has been sheltered. Additionally, adding a cover crop to the soil will boost soil fertility when the crop decomposes after being turned into the soil.

- **Annual cover crops should be planted**

Annual cover crops, such as annual ryegrass, red clover, and hairy vetch, might benefit your raised bed garden if sown at the end of the growing season. They supply nutrients to the soil, especially if dug into the bed in the spring, decrease erosion, and fix nitrogen in the soil in the case of vetch and clover.

- **Make a beautiful edible garden.**

Even the most basic raised bed can be transformed into a lovely garden destination. Plan an aesthetically pleasing arrangement of your favorite edibles, couple them with gorgeous blooming companion plants to attract beneficial insects to the garden, and you'll be able to create a living work of art—while also increasing your harvests. Pollinators will be attracted to the blossoms if you plant flowers along the border of your raised bed, which will help pollinate your crops and enhance harvests. Beneficial predatory insects will also appreciate the blooms, which will aid in the control of pests in the garden.

- **Consider planning ahead to extend the season**

With a little forethought ahead of time, you may start growing earlier in the season or stretch your growing season well into the fall. Installing supports for a basic low tunnel or cold frame will save you time and effort when it's time to shield your crops from frost.

- **Critter management**

One of the advantages of having a raised bed in your yard is keeping track of the animals that eat and destroy your precious plants. Have you ever raised huge, red tomatoes on the vine, allowing them to get redder and riper on the vine, only to discover one morning that some picky creature has taken a bite out of it, spit it out, and moved on to explore what else is on offer at your backyard buffet?

Choose disease-resistant plants that aren't attracted to animals and insects to keep your beds low-maintenance. Use fertile soil, the correct quantity of fertilizer, irrigation, and light or shade to keep your garden healthy. Plants with comparable requirements should be grouped together.

Try organic methods first, such as barriers, a good blast from the hose, or sprays manufactured from non-toxic home goods, before turning to pesticides (which are often the final choice).

- **Gophers, moles, and ground squirrels** are underground scavengers who eat bulbs and shoots by tunneling under the earth. Place root balls in wire cages or line planting holes with hardware cloth barriers if this happens in your raised bed.
- **Snails and slugs.** Enclose vegetable and flower plots

with 3-inch-high copper bars. When a snail or slug contacts copper, it receives a little electrical shock, which causes it to flee (not enough to kill it). Another option is to fill a shallow bowl with beer and dig a small hole flush with the top of the soil, flooding the bowl's lip with the soil. Snails and slugs are drawn to the beer and will swim in it, drowning.
- **Flying and crawling insects:** Use gauze to protect vegetable leaves from flying and crawling insects. It's available at garden centers and on the internet.

Raised bed gardening can be a great way to create a garden when space is limited. It is a fun, efficient, and easy to maintain way to exercise your green thumb. So, take the time to look at the options available to you and start your own raised vegetable garden today.

Printed by Libri Plureos GmbH in Hamburg, Germany